THE PURSUIT OF
GOVERNANCE

THE PURSUIT OF GOVERNANCE

*Nordic Dispatches on a
New Middle Way*

FABRIZIO TASSINARI

agenda
publishing

For Mirko

© Fabrizio Tassinari 2022

First published in 2022 by Agenda Publishing

Agenda Publishing Limited
The Core
Bath Lane
Newcastle Helix
Newcastle upon Tyne
NE4 5TF
www.agendapub.com

ISBN 978-1-78821-400-1 (hardcover)
ISBN 978-1-78821-401-8 (paperback)

British Library Cataloguing-in-Publication Data
A catalogue record for this book is available from the British Library

Typeset by JS Typesetting Ltd, Porthcawl, Mid Glamorgan
Printed and bound in the UK by CPI Group (UK) Ltd, Croydon, CR0 4YY

Contents

"For it is only by reconciling contradictions that
power can be retained indefinitely."
Emmanuel Goldstein

Acknowledgements

This book is "autobibliographical", in the sense that it relies heavily on the vast governance literature, as much as on real-life encounters and observations drawn from over a decade of living and working in Europe's North. As a result, the notes are meant to give reference to facts and quotations, or to indicate where I have drawn directly on a secondary source for insight. Otherwise, this work has relied on a number of extraordinary individuals, without whom the book would not have been possible.

From an enlightened diplomat, Nanna Hvidt, I learned everything I know about Nordic leadership, especially the Danish saying: "Put ice in your stomach", with which she once scolded me during a dispute with the Danish far right (which objected to being called "far right"). I thank Lars Vissing for permitting me to take up some of the theses we wrote about together on Renaissance diplomacy, of which he is one of the world's foremost authorities. I also thank him for letting me drive his Lancia Flaminia Superleggera, which brought a little bit of the 1950s Italian miracle through the streets of Copenhagen. Wherever I am, the Danish Institute for International Studies, where this book was first conceived, and Denmark as a whole, will always feel like the home I come back to.

I thank Professor Bernd Henningsen, founding director of the NordEuropa-Institut at Humboldt University in Berlin. Not only has Bernd been a mentor to me for the better part of the last two decades; he advocated for the German government's Humboldt Foundation award that enabled me to write much of this book. I thank the Berggruen Institute in Los Angeles for the generous support it has given to finish this project, and in particular to Nathan Gardels, with whom over the years I have found a rare meeting of minds.

Steve Jobs once said that in life "you can only connect the dots looking backwards", explaining in hindsight why you ended up doing what you did. Four years ago, I found myself setting up a new School of Transnational Governance at the European University Institute in Florence. The School is a compelling project, into which I have put many of the values that I describe in this book. I am especially grateful to Renaud Dehousse and Miguel Maduro for having taught me the profession of "institution builder." I thank the staff, the faculty and the students, who put up with my Nordic idiosyncrasies on a daily basis. I now find myself working with Alex Stubb, former prime minister of Finland, and Mario Monti, former prime minister of Italy, respectively dean and board chairman of the School, whom I have read and heard on these issues for years.

I am grateful to my parents, who ironically raised me in a Roman neighbourhood named after Nordic playwrights (in our case, Strindberg Square), and who unwittingly inspired the case study of diamonds. The completion of this book was in many ways a labour of love at a time of pandemic lockdown. That exceptional situation made it apparent, if ever it was needed, that Marie and William are my only North Star.

ACKNOWLEDGEMENTS

This book is dedicated to the memory of Mirko, my beloved little brother, who suddenly passed away in the Fall of 2020.

Fabrizio Tassinari
Florence/Berlin

Introduction: the pioneers

The Nordics have their own Alexis de Tocqueville. In the 1930s, a young American correspondent and later Pulitzer Prize-winning journalist named Marquis Childs undertook a journey to Sweden to examine the bold new experiment being pursued there in offering a cradle-to-grave welfare state. Not unlike Tocqueville, the nineteenth-century French diplomat whose *Democracy in America* captured the spirit of the nascent United States, Childs's account of the emergent Nordic social model produced an unlikely classic entitled *Sweden: The Middle Way* (1936).

Against the background of a looming struggle between fascism and democracy, capitalism and communism, Childs' short book chronicled the ways in which effective democratic governance could overcome ideological confrontation and deliver results. Through a detailed study of the cooperative system, Childs demonstrated how Sweden, and the Nordics by extension, fared between the "concentration of economic power in the hands of a few men" in the United States and "the trials and hardships in Russia". While firmly in the Western camp, Sweden had somehow managed to intercept and absorb the revolutionary winds blowing from the East. The subtitle – *The Middle Way* – would become a cliché of centrist politics.

The book made a splash. At the time, the *New York Herald Tribune* reviewed it enthusiastically: "[It] reads like the best political news in years. [It] sounds gloriously like what we used to think of as American: a method of sane compromise and steady progress, each step tested by the sole criterion: does it work?"[1] US President Franklin Delano Roosevelt, in the midst of that most ambitious of middle-way kind of experiment, the New Deal, sent a delegation to Sweden. He reasoned thus:

> I became a good deal interested in the cooperative development in countries abroad, especially Sweden. A very interesting book came out a couple of months ago – *The Middle Way*. I was tremendously interested in what they had done in Scandinavia along those lines. In Sweden, for example, you have a royal family and a Socialist Government and a capitalist system, all working happily side by side. Of course, to be sure, it is a smaller country than ours; but they have conducted some very interesting and, so far, very successful experiments. They have these cooperative movements existing happily and successfully alongside of private industry and distributions of various kinds, both of them making money. I thought it was at least worthy of study from our point of view.[2]

There is no overt ideological battle in the twenty-first century. Yet, citizens at every latitude register growing dissatisfaction with the results delivered by their governments. In the West, they increasingly turn to populist forces to seek an easy respite to the frustration caused by the failures of democracy.

Other models of governance, such as China's "autocratic capitalism", rest on technocratic command and control methods that are disdained in the West, but whose global appeal is growing mostly due to their perceived ability to deliver. No matter where and how they are practiced, these alternatives seem to offer only partial and unsatisfactory answers to increasingly complex questions of governance. In a world ravaged by pandemics and climate crises, migration flows and cyberwars, rigid rule-making imparted from above or populist over-simplifications brewing from below can only represent the extremes of a more sophisticated picture of governing processes.

To the extent that liberal democracy has so far weathered wars and financial collapse, epidemics and natural disasters, it is because of its "practical" ability to adjust, adapt and balance two of the most innate aspirations of our species. On the one hand, it has sought to fulfill our quest for liberty: it has enabled individual freedom to be protected under the rule of law, human rights, suffrage and representation – all in the pursuit of humanity's ultimate Holy Grail, happiness, which the American founding fathers so indelibly inscribed in the Declaration of Independence. On the other hand, democratic governance has fulfilled our need for security: it has enabled humans to exit the caves of their state of nature to pursue survival by means of cooperation; our quest for security has turned into solidarity and ultimately welfare and prosperity.

The nexus of liberty and security is imperfect and malleable, interpreted and accented in different ways depending on where one lives. In some cases, democracies place more emphasis on liberty, while in others, they prioritize creating a safety net for their citizens. The nexus is mutually reinforcing. More security has expanded the horizon of liberty: with increasing safety, we have gradually felt more at ease to open borders and lower barriers rather than to lock ourselves up. More liberty has brought more security: the vision of democratic peace rendering war among democracies impossible.

Yet in recent years, this nexus has been questioned head-on. Whether because of an uncontrolled influx of refugees or a deadly virus, whether it is the presidency of Donald Trump in the United States or Brexit in the United Kingdom, the pursuit of security and of liberty are being radicalized and decoupled: states are closing up in an attempt to protect their citizens. Border closures seem to be the Pavlovian response to any crisis. An irreversible securitization of the public discourse has traded the explanation of complexities with the alarm of a constant emergency. The pursuit of liberty and security is being pulled to the point of breaking their nexus altogether.

This book argues that virtuous polities in the twenty-first century are still searching for a middle way. Like in Childs' intuition, this new middle way is a mindset, a "practical" one that should be tested against the sole criterion: "does it work?". What matters to citizens are the outcomes and the effects of governance: whether these are measured in the quality of our bus rides, school roofs, number of ICU beds in our hospitals, or more generally our well-being, both of the material and immaterial sort. Unlike in Childs' story, policy makers today are no longer looking for ideological lodestars between left and right, capitalism and socialism. They are, in a sense, grappling with their skewed byproducts and scrambling for a workable equilibrium between liberty and security. They are looking for formulas that can help them navigate more complex and often seemingly incompatible dichotomies in the methods, cultures and practices of governance. The middle way in the twenty-first century relates to governance: it is one that balances the technocratic processes deeply embedded in the ways mature states operate, with the populist insurgency that increasingly challenge them.

Only by reconciling these most basic instincts present in our body politic, can we lay out the future conditions of governance. Admittedly, governance is a difficult beast to capture: it concerns our practices of governing, but also the results that these produce. It relates to the state, as the primary unit of analysis and policy action; but it increasingly spans beyond the local and the regional all the way to the global and planetary levels. As a result, governance is analysed through an increasingly sophisticated prism of theories, sources and methods; measured by quantitative indicators and qualitative surveys about the policies that are formulated.[3] More often still, good governance is a totemic reference used and abused in the discourse of zealous administrators desperate to contain the populist rage. It refers to how authority is exercised, controlled, legitimized and ultimately to the values that guide us as individuals and communities.

This book does not hold the ambition to reinvent governance or its principles; nor does it wish to dissemble democracy and its institutions. More precisely, it sets out to investigate how governance can again satisfy the legitimate demands of effects by citizens, by asking whether and how democratic governments can again deliver public goods. While I will not question the real or imagined fallacies of the liberal world order, I ask whether and how the nexus of liberty and security can be repaired and reinforced in order to produce again results.

When results are not forthcoming, sometimes it is useful to look elsewhere to find them: in my case, the Nordics. For the purists, "Scandinavian" and "Nordic" do not mean the same thing. The former relates to Norway, Sweden and Denmark, and their linguistic and historical commonality, while the latter includes also Finland and Iceland. But for the arguments expounded upon in this book, they are at times used interchangeably to refer to the place on Earth where democratic governance has delivered some of its most notable effects, and the place where I lived and worked for over a decade at the crossroads of academia and policy.

To the outsider's perception, the North is a geographical frontier, made of unforgiving weather and dark winters, the place where "the snowflakes storm, when the rivers freeze and summer ends", as sung by a young Bob Dylan and Johnny Cash in "Girl from the North Country". In more erudite iterations, the "Nordic model" is some kind of existential frontier: it is a welfare state paradise, made of universal healthcare and free education – a "fortunate land"[4] in the words of Marquis Childs and the El Dorado of US left-wing senator Bernie Sanders' "democratic socialism".

In more than one way, Northern Europe is an outlier, which tops all sorts of global rankings with such consistency, as to seem almost incongruous: from competitiveness to equality, from transparency to social mobility and, indeed, happiness. The Nordics are the metonymy of a virtuous society, which many would like to inhabit, of a polity that anticipates trends and that every country would like to imitate.[5] In my case, the Nordic experience is all of the above, but it is also a reference point to unpack practices and experiences of democratic governance and to sketch a future that concerns us all.

It is not a hopeless aspiration: after the Great Recession of 2008, several observers and analysts have understandably taken inspiration from Europe's North to find clues about democracy's renewal. Scholars such as Francis Fukuyama and organizations such as the World Bank even coined a phrase, "Getting to Denmark",[6] as shorthand for good governance. The association of Nordic governments with social justice and sustainability, of a profound symbiosis of the state with its citizens, is almost axiomatic.

To be fair, there are no models to emulate: cultural backgrounds, historical and social dynamics cannot be seamlessly transplanted from country to country. In the methodology of the social sciences, however, single case-study research is precisely made of extreme and exceptional circumstances that can help extrapolate general theses. In an era of growing inequality and the ever-gnawing gap between elites and the people, state and companies, the Nordics are the kind of extreme case that can help to draw the contours of the possible future of governance.

It is not only my conviction: after a trip to Sweden in the 1960s, the American cultural critic Susan Sontag wrote that "what happens here, will happen five or ten or fifteen years in some other part of the advanced world".[7] Nordics like to call themselves *foregangslande*, pioneers. Perhaps because these nations are small, wealthy and until recently ethnically homogeneous, they have managed to experiment and anticipate before others. This experimentation embodies how liberal democracy delivers good governance. Europe's North has perfected and constantly reinvented the nexus of individual freedom and collective security. While many excellent books have concerned themselves with the future of liberal democracy and several often single out the Nordics as a case for emulation, I will embark on the opposite journey, taking the Nordics as a point of departure to tease out some principles and draw some broader conclusions about the future of governance.

In this respect, being an outlier also comes with a dark side. By focusing on practices and effects of governance, I seek to unpack why the same reasons that have made the Nordics "pioneers" have brought with them some of the most degenerative sides of governance. By contextualizing the forces that are pulling liberty and security in two opposite directions, I explain why the Nordic experience exemplifies also the mutation, at once terrifying and inevitable, of democratic governance in the twenty-first century: morphing the nexus of liberty and security into one between populism and technocracy.

This book is organized in three concentric circles: the nucleus is the nation-state. It frames the *method* of governance by overviewing the spectrum of possible, different modes, and how the Nordic experience has effectively moved across them (Chapter 1). From that basis, the focus shifts to the *sources* of governance. I will explain how the Nordics managed to strike a middle ground between elites and people, by means of that which they call the "conversation" (Chapter 2).

The next circle is continental and takes off from the divide between Northern and Southern Europe in order to tease out the historical and geographical fault lines in the *culture* of governance, in Europe and beyond (Chapter 3). Subsequently, the analysis moves on to the all-important question of the institutions sustaining governance practices and policies, that which I call the *scaffolding* of governance. To exemplify its importance, I will focus on the case of labour-market reforms in Southern and Northern Europe (Chapter 4).

The third circle is global and zooms in on the *limitations* of governance in a world made of a complex web of relations among states, supranational institutions, business, civil society and media (Chapter 5). Next, I focus on the *practices* of global governance in the twenty-first century that can repair the fractures created by this growing complexity. Beginning with the case of the diplomacy of blood diamonds and ending with climate governance, I propose a model of institutional design that can successfully address the complexity that this (dis)order has generated (Chapter 6). The book concludes by spelling out the paradox of governance that even a virtuous case such as the Nordic region lays bare: the need for a new consensus to be found between control, rule-making and ultimately technocracy, on the one hand, and legitimacy, differentiation, and ultimately populism on the other, with the aim to recompose and renew the nexus of liberty and security.

The Nordic countries routinely register the world's highest levels of life satisfaction.[8] Alexander Stubb, a former prime minister of Finland, once told me that this is because their pursuit of happiness has evolved into one of "meaning". In a similar vein, this book argues that this pursuit derives, at least in part, from the place that each of us occupies in a peaceful and free community. It sets to spell out the method of this pursuit, the practices into which it translates, and the limitations that it encounters. Above all, I hope that it will portray a kind of future that can be meaningful for the rest of us.

1

From Singapore to Sacramento: a method of governance

These being the most influential 300 square-feet in the whole country, they look remarkably frugal. The lamps and ubiquitous candles form a choreography of asymmetric shadows on the pastel-coloured walls. If it were not for the copies of local and international dailies scattered on the mid-century teak desk, it would be hard to guess that this is the office of the editor-in-chief of the most important newspaper in the country.

I am about to be seated on one of two opposing dark-brown leather armchairs next to the desk, and I ask to have a glimpse of the majestic view from the corner office onto Copenhagen City Hall Square. Alas, I do not get to breathe any of the self-importance I had anticipated: the square has been transformed into a gigantic crater for the construction of a new subway line. It has been a frustratingly long project, marred with delays and minor accidents. Most Danes are fed up with the Italian contractors widely blamed for the blunders – even though afterwards they are immensely proud of the unmanned metroline they have delivered. "I really can't say", answers the soft-spoken secretary with a smile, when I ask when they will be finished.

Before serving at the helm of *Politiken*, Denmark's leading daily, Bo Lidegaard had done most other things. A career diplomat, he was a top advisor of successive prime ministers and embodies the glorious technocratic tradition that sustains democratic institutions in Europe's North. As a historian, he has chronicled the origins and development of the modern Danish state and the life of some of its most defining statesmen. His best-known book *Countrymen* recounted the story of the rescue of Danish Jews in 1943, and was a bestseller translated into several languages. His name does not appear on the ballot paper (though the surname does, as Lidegaard's younger brother was Denmark's foreign minister). Yet this diverse background makes him something of a polymath of Danish democracy.

Newspaper editors are legendary for their short attention-span and even shorter fuse. So precious is time in blue-chip journalism, that the *Financial Times* at one point offered one-to-one chats with the editors in end-of-year charity auctions at Christie's. Here I did not have to bid in order to obtain a full 45-minute conversation starting with the origins of modern Scandinavian statehood in the nineteenth century. Cultivated, patrician, Lidegaard wears the uniform of Nordic intelligentsia: black blazer, white button-down shirt, no tie, and dark jeans, which are unmarked but betray the cut of some refined designer. He moves effortlessly across historical eras and academic disciplines with an overarching narrative of civic responsibility, where enlightened elites were instrumental to the creation of the modern welfare state.

I am here to talk about the specificities and lessons of what he calls the "most competitive social model on earth".[1] When asked the secret of Nordic success, Lidegaard does not blink:

"the cashier at Netto", he explains, referring to a local discount supermarket chain, "has the same creed as the civil servant". "Creed" is a loaded term but Lidegaard does not use it casually. It is a reflection of the almost religious reverence to the social contract in this part of the world.

When I hear this, I am reminded of Karl Popper, the Austrian-British philosopher who was said to disdain of the likes of Lidegaard. Plato called them "philosopher kings" and Popper thought they were imbued with a dangerous messianism that entitles them to try out highly questionable experiments of "social engineering" – an accusation often leveled at the intrusive government institutions in Northern Europe. In this case, even in egalitarian Scandinavia, it is increasingly questionable that a supermarket cashier, whose shifts are being shortened because of automation and whose suburban supermarket is visited time and again by desperate, and often foreign, shoplifters, shares the worldview concocted by civil servants sipping coffee in dimly-lit, pastel-coloured ministerial rooms, almost identical to Lidegaard's office.

Precisely because of this contrast, it is important to pin down what this "creed" is all about. In what follows I shall set out a method of governance rooted in social constructivism and show how even Marquis Childs' original "middle way" was unwittingly rooted in it. I shall then tease out the conceptual spectrum along which different governance experiences have positioned themselves. I conclude by showing how the Nordic example has pragmatically shifted and moved across this continuum by comparing the cases of the Danish and Swedish government responses to the Covid-19 pandemic since March 2020.

Seizing the middle way

Marquis Childs did not know it, but he was a constructivist. When categorizing Sweden as the "middle way", he must have instinctively felt that "anarchy", as international relations scholar Alexander Wendt wrote in his seminal study of social constructivism, "is what states make of it".[2] Constructivism, in this respect, is not a theory as such, but a theory of knowledge,[3] shaded according to how social reality displays itself. There is probably not even one single constructivist methodology; it is rather the practice of uncovering how social facts unfold. Had Sweden in fact veered towards "democratic socialism", as Americans erroneously label it today, Childs would have probably picked another subtitle or another case. The key methodological insight of the middle way is that it is the exact opposite of finding a new label, a new category; it is about positioning and indeed constructing a social reality.

This goes to the heart of social science epistemology. The debate within it has perennially swung between exclusive acceptance or total rejection of social phenomena as "brute facts".[4] Rationalists claim that social facts are irrefutable: objectivity, positivism and determinism are their defining traits. Interpretative approaches instead argue that facts as such do not exist; power originates from ideas and consequently the creation of knowledge is an eminently subjective affair. Much like in Childs' intuition, constructivism rejects this dialectic framing. The very same phenomenon can be examined from different perspectives and can produce different interpretations.

It is not by chance that international relations scholar Emmanuel Adler speaks about constructivism as "seizing the middle ground". Different interpretations can be placed along a continuum, each possessing their own validity and coherence. Attempting to combine idealism and realism, then, would be tantamount to mixing water and oil. Constructivism "is not anti-liberal or anti-realist by ideological conviction; neither is it pessimistic or optimistic by design".[5] What it does is to "dot the margin" of the analysis, says Norwegian political scientist Iver Neumann.[6] And much like in the study of cooperatives in Sweden in the 1930s, this margin is dotted by scrutinizing social facts according to how they display themselves. Childs observed reality first, then deliberated. He starts out by saying that the world is ravaged by ideology and then observed social facts much like one would observe a natural phenomenon. He does not draw conclusions before observing how reality unfolds.

A corollary to this argument is that no deliberation is possible for facts that have yet to take place. This explains why Stephen Walt, for one, defines constructivism as "agnostic" and "better at describing the past than anticipating the future".[7] At the same time, the construction of social reality is a continuous process of learning. It allows the establishment of a connection between the origin of social facts, their unfolding and their possible future developments, what is also known as cognitive evolution. Cognitive evolution, according to Adler, means that "at any point in time and place of historical process, institutional or social facts may be socially constructed by collective understandings of the physical and the social world that are subject to authoritative (political) selection processes and thus to evolutionary change".[8] Based on a reading of the reality in the past and the present, observation is equipped to indicate possible scenarios for the future.

In this reading, that young, intrepid American journal-ist travelling across Scandinavia in the middle of the Great Depression was a constructivist *ante litteram*. He did not take sides between socialism and capitalism; it might be more appropriate to say that while acknowledging their existence, he literally sidelined them, placed them on the opposite extremes of a continuum of analysis, a container in which contrasting approaches and different ideologies are placed. The synthesis that he created does not aim at subsuming or mediating between the extremes; nor does it adhere a priori to any of them; rather, it aimed to comprise them, to "dot the margins".

This choice presents an inescapable ethical dilemma for any observer. In this age of social media echo chambers, we tend to overlook that the role of the analyst is to observe and report what political, social and economic actors do. Yet, one might as well acknowledge upfront that no observation is a politically neutral act. While analysts and reporters should not take sides, they ought to take responsibility for the awk-ward position they are in. Much like in today's heated envi-ronment of "fake news" and "mainstream media", it is of the essence that analysts possess the moral clarity of acknowl-edging the difference between analysis and advocacy and of any involuntary and yet inevitable bias therein.[9]

What Childs did was to report on what Swedish social, economic and political actors were doing. In fact, an analysis swinging perpetually along a continuum between socialism and capitalism would have been toothless and perhaps point-less, if it did not draw any operative conclusions about how to take our understanding of reality forward. And in this, Childs was unquestionably sympathetic to the Scandinavian model.

Put another way: there will be competing discourses about governance and democracy. Within those, there will always be some dominant or hegemonic ones, "nodal points" as Ernesto Laclau and Chantal Mouffe call them.[10] Moral clarity is essentially about doing due diligence: acknowledging one's limitations and biases and then settling somewhere for the purpose of delivering workable outcomes.

Once we have uncovered and defused the ideological land-mines on which social analysis can fall, we can more safely look at how reality unfolds. Here "cognitive evolution" takes a very practical meaning: we learn from experience, real existing instances in which good governance not only took place but can serve an explanatory purpose for the future. Much like Childs, the method of this analysis will be to witness virtuous practices that can serve as case studies to answer broader questions about the future "when the investigator has little control over events".[11]

By picking a case study that was unique and critical, Childs was unwittingly picking a signpost, something at once extreme and constitutive of the bigger story he wanted to tell about an uncertain future. I shall do much the same in this book. I rely on a number of critical, and seemingly disparate, in-depth, single case studies. On that basis, I articulate how actors operate, the way they talk and act social reality into existence, their "speech acts".[12] By unearthing the constructivist inspiration and biases of the original "middle way", I shall thus chart a path for virtuous and less virtuous practices in the contemporary governance landscape.

Thus swung the pendulum

"The expansion of the right of the individual to behave or misbehave as he pleases has come at the expense of orderly society" once argued Lee Kwan Yew, Singapore's founding prime minister and patriarch: "In the East, the main object is to have a well-ordered state and not in a natural state of contention and anarchy". He continues: "First you must have order in society ... Then the schools, when you have violence in schools, you are not going to have education, so you've got to put that right. Then you have to educate rigorously and train a whole generation of skilled, intelligent, knowledgeable people who can be productive".[13]

Singapore is arguably the world's most sophisticated technocracy, and these are the kind of statements that have earned Lee a rock-star reputation ever since he stepped down as Singapore's prime minister in 1990. He has been compared to other great statesmen; former US president Richard Nixon once claimed that had Lee lived in Britain, he would have reached "the world stature of a Churchill, a Disraeli, or a Gladstone". While he ruled his people with an iron fist more akin to that of some authoritarian regimes, it is hard to not sympathize with some of his concerns about democracy.

The crux of the matter, familiar at one point or another to any Western leader, is how you can accumulate the authority necessary to push through painful reforms without losing popularity and, eventually, the legitimacy to do so. Here culture plays a role, if it is true that Asian culture emphasizes "the values of patron-client communitarianism, personalism, deference to authority, dominant political parties, and strong interventionist states".[14] As a result of this, the complex thrust-and-parry characterizing the art of governing is moderated by an intricate web of clientelistic relations and a myriad of intermediate bureaucratic, business and non-governmental bodies, which are tasked with filtering through decisions and helping to execute them.

Lamenting the historical failure of social democracy, the British historian Tony Judt wrote that: "for most people, most of the time, the legitimacy and credibility of a political system rests not on the liberal practices or democratic forms but upon order and predictability ... above all, we want to be safe".[15] Seen in this light, this is exactly what East Asian governance practices have prioritized. On a continuum ranging from liberty to security, they placed their bets squarely at the security end.

As extensively discussed by political theorists,[16] this choice is favoured by the fact that Asian-style governance is based on paternalism and hierarchy; traditions and religions defer status and authority to personal "karma", and put stability ahead of freedom. The Confucian pursuit of harmony is at the polar opposite to the American pursuit of happiness. In fact, the values that we traditionally associate with liberal democracy take individual freedom as their point of departure. In Asia, the starting point is relational: how people, groups and productive sectors relate to each other in such way as to uphold public order.

Now swing the pendulum across the globe. America was never meant to occupy the other end of the governance spectrum, but it has gradually emerged as Asia's mirror image. Indirect democracy is premised on the assumption that voters delegate their decisions, and indeed their best intentions, to elected assemblies. As Edmund Burke put it: "Your representative owes you, not his industry only but his judgment; and he betrays instead of serving you if he sacrifices it to your opinion". American founding fathers were also preoccupied with ensuring that minorities were represented and would not be subject to the majority's yoke, while at the same time not have the power to hold majorities hostage by their veto. Precisely because of this, the essence of representative democracy is in the ability to mediate and, where possible, reconcile conflicting positions.

The past half century, however, has witnessed a gradual erosion of this elaborate system of checks and balances. Political scientists recognize well a mechanism that gets small groups to pursue special interests. Lobby groups are a modern-day incarnation of what Italian Renaissance philosopher Francesco Guicciardini called *il particulare*, "the particular", the special interests that come before the common aspirations binding a community. *Particulare*, mind you, is not the same as saying "partisan". Someone could be partisan and still hold a worldview that is aimed at serving the interests of a plurality, if not a majority of people. The essence of democratic governance is precisely the ability to listen to, and if applicable incorporate, opposing partisan views.

On the contrary, a most severe dysfunction of the democratic process arises when the act of delegation to representatives morphs into a marketization of power. That can be deduced just by observing the last two decades during which the United States has oscillated from a war-mongering George W. Bush administration and the isolationism of the Tea Party, to an idealistic one under Barack Obama, to the disruptive and destructive Donald Trump administration, and back to what, at the time of writing, looks like a more progressive and pragmatic tenure under Joe Biden. At this point, it might be in order to spend time deciphering the anomaly brought about by Trump's presidency, his disregard for democratic customs and rules, or even the ineptitude that characterized his administration. That goes far beyond the scope of this book. Yet, irrespective of his defeat in the 2020 presidential election, it is hard not to see his presidency as a low point (time will tell if it is a point of non-return) in the chequered journey of democratic governance.

Some of the very undercurrents that brought Trump to power preceded his presidency by at least four decades. They are embodied in the system of ballot propositions which, especially since the 1970s, have disfigured the face of democracy in California. The most familiar landmark of this practice is known as Proposition 13, a 1978 referendum initiative that sanctioned a decrease in property taxes and of revenue for local government institutions. As a result, the Golden State radiating from Sacramento, which up until the 1960s not only produced some of Hollywood's classic movies but also some of the world's best pre-school education systems and public institutions of higher education, was forced to implement drastic cuts, with the maintenance of basic public infrastructure from streets to schools in disarray.

More broadly, Proposition 13 kicked off a metamorphosis of democratic practices. In the 1960s, only 88 referendums had been held throughout the United States; in the 1970s, when California held Prop. 13, no fewer than 181 took place, growing to 257 in the 1980s and 378 in the 1990s. The resort to this form of direct democracy has grown manifold since Prop. 13, producing "a political system that is as close to anarchy as any civilized society has seen".[17]

The political arc of former California governor Jerry Brown is illustrative of this development. A convinced environmentalist and opposer of the death penalty, Brown first became governor in 1975, succeeding Ronald Reagan, on a fiscal conservative platform. Quite soon after his appointment, he found himself dealing with Proposition 13, which he had opposed, and the damage that it inflicted. As a result of the proposition, California was faced with cash shortages, the near impossibility to raise taxes and the need to fund basic services in local districts, including schools, which it did by means of state income taxes and by frittering away a state budget surplus of almost $5 billion.

After a panoply of other positions, the Californian voters amazingly returned Brown as governor in 2011, 30 years after he had left that office, to succeed another action hero, Arnold Schwarzenegger. In his second incarnation, Brown was again confronted head-on with the problematic budget issue. In 2012 he championed Proposition 30, principally aimed at raising revenue tax for top-earners and sales tax. For the first time in almost a decade, Californians voted to raise taxes and they did so to avoid a severe cut in the funding of public education. For Brown, who believes that "the California dream is built on great public schools and colleges and universities", this was crucial.[18] After years of abyss-facing deficits, starting in 2014 California had again a state budget surplus of $4.2 billion.

So what is the takeaway of these snapshots on Jerry Brown and Lee Kwan Yew? They are diametrically opposed, geographically and intellectually: the former responding, adapting, bowing to the primacy of freedom; the other abiding, enforcing, and even glorifying that of security. The first had to face the ultimate consequences of California's wild individualism, the latter has created a nearly martial hierarchy of government. Brown is no more Nordic than Lee, which is to say that neither of them is. Even so, their clear-eyed approach to public policy, "a relentless pursuit of the possible and a serene neglect of everything else",[19] as *The Economist* described the politics of Brown's second gubernatorial term, has a remarkable assonance with the pragmatism that makes Europe's North tick.

More than that, between the two of them, they virtually cover the extremes of the whole spectrum of governance options, as we have come to know them: from Singapore's rigorously technocratic decision-making to California's populist marketization of direct democracy. It would be far-fetched to claim that half-way between Singapore and Sacramento, there exists a real place that combines elements of both. Yet the Nordic experience with governance has found a way to stand squarely between them.

Political bricolage

Marquis Childs' argument, in the middle of the most severe recession of the modern era and with a brewing ideological confrontation between East and West, was evidently appealing. There is no obvious reason why solidarity and social security should not be compatible with individual liberties and the unbridled spirits of capitalism. Scandinavia occupied a niche where there indeed existed two opposing worldviews.

In fact, rather than standing between capitalism and socialism, it would be more accurate to claim that the Nordics embraced both. Time and again, when the world economies retrenched in protectionism, Europe's North has stood out for its openness to trade; when Wall Street capitalism pushed America into free-wheeling deregulation, the Nordics expanded healthcare provision, free education, "to check", as Childs put it, "the very tendencies by which capitalism tends to destroy itself".[20] Private actors and the state join forces in innovative ways, whenever it was needed and because it worked: whether it is to extend infrastructure to remote areas, conserve and extract natural resources, or build efficient and affordable housing projects. All of this, as FDR intuited, earning money, to the extent that Swedish GDP per capita between 1870 and 1964 grew fastest in the world, bar Japan.

Childs' reportage is not a hagiography of a socialist utopia, idyllic and faultless; it is a story of rough competition and financial acumen, hostile takeovers and unmitigated survival of the fittest. "A long, long struggle for existence", he writes, "toughened the Scandinavians. For centuries they warred with each other; with half the nations of Europe; and always with a land for the most part bleak and harsh. The sagas of the Vikings are proof that they had, to start with, tenacity, price and a fierce kind of bravery".[21]

In a sense, the middle way never really existed. Childs did not theorize an alternative path between East and West. There was no balancing act between opposing ideologies, or clash of civilizations, not to mention a worldview that could subsume socialism and capitalism. The middle way stood out as a sort of political bricolage, an artisanal do-it-yourself operation where some enlightened policy entrepreneurs tinkered with what they found in society, and put it together with the only purpose to make it work. In Childs' view, the Nordic middle way was "above all in their willingness to adjust, to compromise, to meet what appears to be reality. They have not been bound by a 'system', nor have they been committed to a dogma. In a sense they are the ultimate pragmatists, interested only in the workability of the social order".[22]

Then as now, the glue of this model is in the culture of consensus and a mindset of compromise. Where I come from, in Italy, compromise has acquired negative connotations: compromise is weak, boneless, the result is flip-flopping, sell-out. If you compromise, it is because you have lost a little bit of dignity. In Europe's North, compromise is overwhelmingly positive. Childs mused: "between the right of the individual and the imperative demands of a complex society; between extreme dry and extreme wet; between those who would exploit every human need and desire for the sake of profit and those who would compel human beings to fit into an arbitrary pattern".[23] "Maybe we don't meet exactly in the middle", Bo Lidegaard, the newspaper editor, told me, "maybe it is 30 per cent you and 70 per cent me", but the result is acceptable for both.

The Swedish language has a word for this, "*lagom*", which encapsulates their philosophy of a life that refuses excesses, the search for the right measure between what is too much and what is too little, and in doing so embodies more than any other word the mindset of these nations. Nordics tend to be realistic about their expectations and find balance in moderation. *Lagom* is literally the mindset of the middle way. This matter-of-fact disposition was once captured with surgical precision by Karl Kristian Steincke, a Danish social reformer of the 1920s. A society, he stated, must be "humane but not soft, democratic but not demagogic, a blend of radical and conservative so far as is necessary if we are not to end in reaction ... It would distinguish itself both from the bleeding-heart sentimentalism that is so nauseating and from the ice-cold rationality that is so chilling".[24]

The middle way narrative that characterized Nordic politics since the 1930s found its best expression in the Swedish *Folkhemmet*, the "people's home". The idea was best formulated by iconic Swedish Prime Minister Per Albin Hannson in 1928. "Per Albin", recounts Childs: "had come to be a symbol of the middle way. In his deliberateness, his calmness, his refusal to be stampeded, he was the essence of reasonable compromise, which in turn is the essence of Sweden's successful adjustment to the age of technology".[25]

In his view, Sweden had to aim to recreate the community and solidarity typical of a home. "The good home", Per Albin argued, "knows no privilege or neglect, no favorites and no stepchildren ... In the good home, equality, thoughtfulness, cooperation and helpfulness prevail".[26] *Folkhemmet* came to epitomize the Nordic welfare state during a four-decade-long period, starting in the early 1930s, traversing almost unscathed the Second World War, and ending in the aftermath of the oil shock of 1973, when Social Democrats held uninterrupted power in Sweden. A similar trajectory applied also to Denmark and Norway, with the key difference that the war and Nazi occupation in those two countries left much deeper scars.

A trademark of the *Folkhemmet* was its bipartisanship. In Denmark in 1933, this led to its own bold version of middle way-politicking, masterminded by Prime Minister Thorvald Stauning and finalized in a deal – revered in Denmark as the "Kanslergade agreement" – between the Agrarian party, later to become a liberal-conservative party in the continental

26

European tradition, the social liberals and the social democrats. By settling sensitive issues such as workers' rights, subsidies to farmers and the devaluation of the currency, Stauning effectively laid the foundations of the Nordic model of a social welfare state. Similarly, the "Saltsjöbaden agreement", signed by Swedish employers and trade unions in 1938, to this day "provides the basis for Sweden's consensus-driven approach to labour relations and is the bedrock of the much-admired Nordic model of capitalism".[27]

In that respect, the notion of "a people's home" may also crystallize why, in the seminal taxonomy on welfare states conceived by Danish sociologist Gøsta Esping Andersen, Scandinavia stands apart from both the liberalized US model and the continental European model, which is more corporatist and family-based.[28] Any foreigner who has lived long enough in these lands will agree that the Nordic countries are a paragon of a universalist welfare state not only for the quality and quantity of the public services delivered, but also for that impalpable but pervasive feeling that the Nordic state replaces the residual role of the family as a safety net.

As the virtual and yet very real home in which the whole country identifies, Nordic societies are closer than any other advanced nation to what others might understand as "tribe". For sure, the culture that underpins it, its social capital, is what holds it together. As American political scientist Robert Putnam has explained, the primordial experience of social capital was to be found in the medieval communes of Central Italy. In his acclaimed *Making Democracy Work*, Putnam traces the origin and practices of what he calls "civic communities" to medieval Italy. He argues that the advancement of the Southern Italian regime was based upon the constitution issued by its twelfth-century ruler, Frederick II. He notes that "in a Hobbesian world of widespread violence and anarchy ... the imposition of social order was the supreme issue of governance".[29] Conversely, the rise of communes in Central-Northern Italy was based on "primordial social contracts"[30] with the people. While these polities were not democratic, "some system of representation and control ... would secure order: the tranquil and peaceful state of the city".[31] The emergence of a sophisticated bureaucratic machinery, the rise of international commerce, and the invention of basic financial institutions completed the picture.

In the centuries that followed, state-formation throughout continental Europe centralized and institutionalized power, often in divisive and traumatic ways. The roots of democratic governance in the Nordic region are distinctive insofar as they channelled participation and shared power in more consensual ways. In the pre-industrial age, this concerned the emancipation of peasants and a gradual transfer of land from the landowners. Rural nobility weakened as a result, gradually morphed into an urban elite, yet retained clout and power by ensuring loyalty to the crown.[32] Local Lutheran parishes cemented a sense of togetherness and belonging based on norms and values that later translated into strong, homogenous societies. The education of young adults – later known in Denmark as *"folkehøjskoler"*, or free high schools – was a crucial factor in the transformation of the agricultural sector. Add urbanization and the emergence of a proto-industrial proletariat, with workers gradually seizing power through their fair share of class struggle in the early 1900s,[33] and you have the societal structure underpinning the political spectrum of the twentieth century.

The obligatory disclaimer here is that it is not entirely fair to make comparisons among political systems. Left and right mean different things in different countries. Yet, this focus on the social capital goes a long way to explaining the Nordics' willingness to come together and to compromise. How else to explain to an outsider the Nordic practice of minority governments, ruling for years without representing the majority of voters but thanks to the outside support of opposition parties. What is more important, this culture of compromise manifests itself in practices of governing, which in turn translate into concrete outputs and deliverables. Any major agreement of strategic relevance, from environmental legislation and social policy to healthcare and defence, is usually the result of a systematic balancing act between government and opposition, employers and trade unions, left and right. Consensus-building and the ability to compromise makes all the difference between the pursuit of short-term gains and the potential longer-term benefits of enlightened self-interest.

Not everyone was as fascinated with this mindset as Marquis Childs was. For some, this culture is the manifestation of a collective bout of conflict avoidance. Swedes call it "conflictophobia", the phenomenon that Susan Sontag defines as being "uncompetitive without being genuinely cooperative".[34] She thought that the premise to achieve such consensus is not a desire to resolve disagreements but to sweep them under the rug.

Worse still, conflicts are pre-empted by a preordained value set. In other words, it is not civility or pragmatism at the heart of the Nordic experience, but conformism, which defines the social norms necessary to be accepted in society. The extent of haggling can vary but the key assumption when entering a Nordic negotiation is that one must follow the unwritten rules of the game. One must know the difference between that which is perceived to be fair from that which is below the belt. In political terms, that has translated into a hegemony of the traditional parties holding the *"Problemformuleringsprivilegium"*,[35] a mouthful translating roughly as the "privilege to formulate issues". Holding that privilege enables you to move within an accepted perimeter of feasible options. Raising new issues outside that range confines you to political wilderness.

Nordics have time and again accepted this trade-off, in a remarkable act of civic responsibility that is easily mistaken for obedience. In the 1970s, British journalist Roland Huntford, for one, went as far as denouncing Sweden as "new totalitarians".[36] It would be natural, he argued, to view the Swedish experience in light of a socialist dystopia such as that described in George Orwell's *Nineteen Eighty-Four*. But what preoccupied Huntford was not only the dubious "Big Brother" quality of the Nordic state. It was rather its degeneration, the "indifference" to the system, more akin, he said, to Aldous Huxley's *Brave New World*: the spectre of a deranged, techno-political machine in which people willingly surrender personal freedom to an omnipresent Leviathan and entrust it to intrude in the fate of each individual.

The French philosopher Michel Foucault, who spent a disappointing three years in Uppsala, Sweden in his early 30s, seemed to reach a similar conclusion (though probably biased and embittered having seen his PhD dissertation, which would later become the seminal *Madness and Civilization*, rejected): "[In Sweden] a human is but a moving dot, obeying laws, patterns and forms in the midst of a traffic that is more powerful and defeats him/her. In its calmness, Sweden reveals a brave new world where we discover that the human is no longer necessary".[37]

There is consensus, then, but it would be fair to qualify it as "engineered" consensus. Choices are limited and artificial. Political parties, trade unions and companies bring their demands and positions to the negotiating table. But each of them contains the seeds of agreement, as they all share the same overarching mindset about what the end goal might look like. On the back of this support, policies and decisions are often imbued with a frighteningly messianic purpose, leading to abominable excesses of social engineering, such as the mass sterilization of disabled people, authorized in Sweden in the name of eugenics. The state knows what is right and seeks to, as the Swedish economist Gunnar Myrdal put it, "protect the citizens against themselves".[38]

These critical voices corroborate the impressions that the Nordics settled on a trade-off between individual liberty and collective security that other Western countries would find unacceptable. Their willingness to accept state authority as legitimate and effective to address individual concerns is in some ways more akin to Singapore than to California. Yet, it cannot be underestimated the extent to which this delegation of authority is a conscious, deliberate act of personal responsibility, which is certainly closer to California than Singapore. Government responses to the Covid-19 pandemic presents a momentous rendering and fitting case study of this hypothesis.

A tale of two pandemics

Ever since March 2020, the Covid-19 pandemic has turned the tables on the global mindset, practices and institutions. Western governments spent a decade debating how centrists could handle the populist rage against immigration and globalization. Covid-19 sorted this dilemma out in a matter of days. For the first time since the Second World War, closing borders was not a choice. In a domino-effect of unilateral national decisions, country after country followed its neighbour in declaring lockdowns, curfews, closed borders and travel bans. Anyone proposing something different was singled out as mad. Suddenly, survival equalled lockdown and quarantines, end of story. No matter how one wishes to explain it, this kind of crisis has determined a short-circuit in the nexus of liberty and security.

At the same time, as Barack Obama put it, "This crisis has reminded us that government matters. It's reminded us that good government matters, that facts and science matter, that the rule of law matters".[39] The capacity of governments to weather the crisis also mattered: the failures of some to tackle the pandemic has mercilessly dented the trust, leadership and operational capacity to deliver public goods – irrespective of whether or not they are democracies.

Consider in this regard the wildly different Nordic responses to the pandemic since March 2020. One might assume that when a cataclysmic crisis such as Covid-19 struck, Nordic countries would be well prepared to respond effectively. However, the evidence is confounding: neighbours such as Sweden and Denmark took drastically different approaches to their pandemic responses, with an implicit quest for herd immunity in the former case and lockdowns in the latter case.

Supposedly very close in their underlying social and political structures, and making decisions on the basis of evidence, science and rigorous public management, Sweden and Denmark nonetheless adopted wildly divergent responses. The incompetence and arrogance that characterized Covid crisis management in authoritarian or populist-run states like Brazil, India and the United States was rightly deplored. Erratic leadership, improvization and hundreds of thousands of deaths present damning indictments of the failures of these regimes. But the performance of supposedly ideally governed countries such as the Nordics has hardly been uniformly strong. By ratcheting up the pressure for rapid response, the pandemic put their well-honed governance mechanisms under stress. It revealed inconsistencies and laid bare some of the most blatant contradictions of democratic governance.

The Danish government was among the first to introduce border closures, travel bans and movement restrictions. This was not a total lockdown as in the case of Italy or Spain; for months after the virus struck, visitors might have been perplexed by the absence of facemasks in most public places. At the same time, Copenhagen introduced some of the most radical border closures and travel restrictions. I was returning from Germany in May 2020, for example, and agents at the Danish border demanded detailed evidence for why I wanted to enter the country that I had called home for the better part of the past two decades. So far-reaching were the measures of Copenhagen's government that the director-general of the Danish Health Authority, Søren Brostrøm, felt compelled to dissociate himself from the travel ban, declaring it a political, rather than scientific, measure.[40]

Prime Minister Mette Frederiksen's justification left little to interpretation: "If we have to wait for evidence-based knowledge in relation to the coronavirus, we will quite simply come too late".[41] The Danish approach involved the imposition of restrictions and the expansion of state authority in ways more reminiscent of places like Taiwan or Singapore that helped flatten the curve of the contagion by means of mass surveillance, contact tracing and stringent quarantine enforcements. When the exit from lockdown was eventually rolled out, most European countries settled on a gradual reopening of industrial activities, aiming to restart disrupted supply chains. Denmark's Social Democrat-led government chose a different tack, reopening kindergartens and elementary schools before anything else, referencing those who could not afford private childcare.

In contrast, Sweden's approach could easily be mistaken for the populist denialism of a Jair Bolsonaro in Brazil or a Donald Trump in the United States. While it enacted a number of targeted closures, such as schools for over-16s, the government in Stockholm deliberately left social life to proceed as normally as possible. Following a mostly volunteer-based approach, the Swedish Prime Minister Stefan Löfven declared: "We who are adults need to be exactly that: adults. Not spread panic or rumors. No one is alone in this crisis, but each person carries a heavy responsibility".[42] With a thinly-veiled reference to the controversial "herd immunity"[43] approach, the Swedish government allowed bars, gyms, shops and restaurants to remain open, counting on a modern and efficient healthcare service to provide protection.

At the same time, it relied on social and cultural habits: even before the Covid-19 contagion hit, an estimated two-thirds of the Swedish population already worked from home at least some of the time, and over half of Swedish households are occupied by one person. As former Prime Minister Carl Bildt joked: "Swedes, especially of the older generation, have a genetic disposition to social distancing". Even so, some observers lambasted Sweden's obstinacy as unconscionable.

The difference in results between the Danish and Swedish approaches has been stark. With over 1,300 Covid-19 deaths per million inhabitants (as of early April 2021), Sweden's toll has been four times higher than Denmark's and about ten times higher than that of Norway or Finland. At the same time, in terms of preventing economic disruption, the results have been slightly worse in Sweden than in Denmark (Sweden's economy contracted by 8.6 per cent and Denmark's by 7.4 per cent in the second quarter of 2020) and worse than in either Norway or Finland. Declines in consumer spending have also been similar in Sweden and Denmark (25 per cent and 29 per cent respectively).[44] While this might seem a damning indictment of the Swedish approach, by the autumn of 2020, the rate of new infections in Sweden was similar to that of Denmark and some other European countries that imposed lockdowns. In the words of Anders Tegnell, the epidemiologist behind Sweden's unusual approach: "In the end, we will see how much difference it will make to have a strategy that's more sustainable, that you can keep in place for a long time, instead of the strategy that means that you lock down, open up and lock down over and over again".[45]

The plethora of "known unknowns" that Covid-19 has unleashed might seem to counsel against drawing premature conclusions. But several months since the start of the pandemic in Europe, it is hard to remain agnostic in the face of data such as the Swedish death rate, which is comparable to countries such as Brazil, whose Covid crisis management has been universally derided. More than that, it is eye-opening to see how Swedish government officials justify these results, with one explaining that staying open was necessary in order for people to be able to continue living a "normal life".[46] One need not be a cynic to conclude that the Swedish government resolved that thousands of mostly elderly casualties were a price worth paying in order to spare the rest of the population from the disruption and uncertainties of a lockdown. This tale of these two Nordic approaches to the coronavirus pandemic shows how similar countries can make dramatically different choices about how to balance the tradeoff between liberty and security.

In a paradoxical way, however, the radically different approaches taken by the Swedish and Danish governments reflect a deeper underlying similarity: these are countries whose populations are among the most trusting in the world. They display an unusual confidence in the state and its institutions. Their respective publics have debated the uses and abuses of scientific evidence, the health costs and the economic consequences. The government's measures did give rise to complaints and objections, especially in Sweden, but there was nothing like the violent protests and rejection of government advice – for example, over the use of personal protective equipment – that over the last year has roiled countries from Germany to the United States.

In the end, the citizens accepted the choice their government made. Citizens, political parties and even the media respected and supported governmental decisions that seemed congruent with technocratic decision-making practices. Social cohesion and trust run so deep that the Swedish and Danish governments might well have swapped their very different Covid-19 strategies and still retained public support.

This ability to move flexibly along the liberty–security spectrum, to adapt and eschew extremes is one of the secrets of the Nordic success. At the same time, the contrasts of the Covid-19 response both reveal what makes up the Nordic model and has laid bare its darker side. When seen in this light, the seemingly libertarian Swedish strategy of managing Covid-19 assumes very different connotations. It is less about voluntarism, responsibility and no lockdowns than about the government, its bureaucracy and its chief epidemiologist deciding how to "protect the citizens against themselves". At the same time, the social trust and organizational capacity underpinning Nordic societies ensures that policies and decisions are the result of painstaking consensus. It is a method of governance that settles for a middle way.

The world emerging from the rubbles of the Covid-19 pandemic has revealed severe limitations even in the best welfare states. The virus has taken millions of lives and perhaps tens of millions of livelihoods. Overcoming this crisis will require all the stamina and resources that we can muster and a fundamental rethink of our lives and the world that we inhabit. Whether or not Covid-19 constitutes an existential threat to liberal democracy, it has offered a unique stress-test of the suitability of our institutions to adapt and withstand shocks.

If there is one overarching lesson to draw from this twin Nordic Covid-19 tale, it is that operational capacity and social trust are crucial assets when addressing the complex challenges of our time. The Nordics remind us that, while the "deep state" may be reviled in some places for its elitist pursuit of control without popular legitimacy, experts and civil servants with the confidence of the people are essential to ensure continuity to policy making. At the same time, when in a pandemic, the end results of high trust and well-governed countries are so divergent and controversial, it is warranted to speculate about the limits of technocracy in delivering effective policy outcomes.

Make no mistake: there is no moral equivalence between technocratic governance and its populist alternative. Covid-19 has confirmed that populists are causing havoc by pandering to our prejudices, mystifying facts and placing established certainties in a state of doubt. But in their attempt to cater to our pursuit of liberty and need for security, even some highly respected governments such as the Nordics have overreached and pushed their policy responses to idiosyncratic excesses.

The defining trait of the Nordic mindset, then, is not technocratic government or social trust; it is compromise, conformism and the spirit of the glass half-full. I have always suspected that this ability to find the middle way and focus on what there is, rather than what there is not, may just be the primary reason why the Nordics top global rankings of the world's happiest nations. The French poet Paul Valéry once wrote: "We hope vaguely, we dread precisely; our fears are infinitely more precise than our hopes".[47] The Nordic governments and its peoples seem to have found a way to hope very precisely.

2

It takes an island: the sources of governance

I have always been fascinated by the repetitiveness of Scandinavian surnames. In the quarter century between 1993 and 2018, three prime ministers followed each other in Denmark, all of them called Rasmussen without being related. This fascination was partly satisfied when I came across a 1965 essay by Carl Henrik Hermanson entitled: *Monopoly and Finance: The Fifteen Families*.[1] The book chronicled in detail the history of the concentration of wealth in Sweden through its most important families, and corroborated my anecdotal impression of being confronted with a tightly-knit elite, which in a small country is inevitably destined to occupy top positions in business, government and cultural institutions.

Having dwelled on the *method* of a middle way governance, the next step of this inquiry will focus on the *sources* of governance: who should we enlist when we seek the new middle way. Known for its egalitarian streak, the Nordic model is in this respect misleading. Even in the fair and equal North, there is a "1%", a plutocracy of individuals that accumulates power and wealth. Unlike in the rest of the Western world, the Nordic elite is not demonized by the remaining 99 per cent: the Jeff Bezoses or Mark Zuckerbergs of this world that earn money even when they are setting up charities[2] are not the target of popular opprobrium.

As elsewhere, the Nordic middle class has been eroded by growing privatization and deregulation. But at least at face value, this has not led to an endemic widening of social and economic divides as experienced in other Western countries.[3] Nor has it erased the centrality of middle management in public and private organizations, with all that that entails in terms of the mobility of individuals growing and rising through the ranks. By the time Marquis Childs grew old in the 1980s, he might have come to witness the "McKinseyfication" of America's economy and society, or what Daniel Markovitz calls the "consulting revolution", which outsourced key public services, in the name of efficiency and shareholder primacy.[4] This would also come to pervade the Nordic countries. As we shall see, the private sector has taken over large swathes of public management, changing the mindset with which critical functions of the state are performed. But it has not led to the hollowing out of the middle class.

Surely, this is partly because the Nordic state has never lost sight of its redistributive function. Progressive taxation goes some way to demonstrating the realization of this priority. But before you wonder, wealth tax has not provided the answer: in a country like Sweden, it was raised for the last time in the 1970s leading some of its more celebrated billionaires like IKEA's founder Ingvar Kamprad to flee to Switzerland, but only to add an estimated 0.4 per cent of GDP. (Wealth and inheritance taxes have since been abolished and "before long, Kamprad returned".[5]) And surely, privatization was made necessary by decades of unbridled expansion of public spending. As scholar Mary Hilson notes: "Scandinavian societies were largely shielded from the worst social effects of the loss of employment in manufacturing by a huge expansion in the public sector, that is, the welfare state and the public bureaucracy required to service it".[6]

But there is something more than meets the eye, which is or should be in fact common to the whole Western experience, and does not relate to taxation or privatization. It is that elites, whether they are economic, political or cultural, are indispensable to the practices of good governance. Any reflection on the sources and resources of governance, especially those that purport to establish a new middle way, should unpack and dissect this claim. In this chapter, I shall start by reviewing how contemporary governance experiences, and especially liberal democracy, have tackled the role of the elites. I posit that elites have historically been entrusted with the task of holding firm the helm of governance because "they know", a phenomenon referred to as "epistocracy". From there, I show how knowledge and education constitute the hallmarks in the acquisition and distribution of power, influence and wealth of healthy governance structures. I shall illustrate how the Nordics have gone about realizing this balance in practice, by zooming in on their experience of summer democracy festivals and what they call the "conversation".

The pincer movement

The road to liberal democracy is the most extraordinary journey that the West has proposed to the world over the past 70 years. A plethora of wildly different cases has persuaded analysts and policy makers to hypothesize that this model of governance was inevitable. From the totalitarian dictatorships defeated in the Second World War and the blood-drenched militarization of Latin America, to the Iberian peninsula after the 1970s, Eastern Europe in the 1980s and 1990s and even North Africa during the past decade: it did seem that a Hegelian "end of history" was nigh indeed.

Yet, getting to democracy has not turned out to be a quiet one-way country road: the travel can be bumpy, it can stop, and as testified by most surveys over the past decade, go into reverse and often back to where it started.[7] Accordingly, our vocabulary on democratic transition, a bit like the one on revolutions, is glittered with attributes: democracy is "managed" as in Russia, "sovereign" as in the Hungarian variant, or generally hyphenated to mark its hybrid and incomplete state. Sub-Saharan Africa and the post-Soviet space have presented paths to democracy that are fake or "virtual", at best. Universal suffrage is formally in place, anywhere from Albania to Zimbabwe; but everywhere you look, there are places where civil liberties and political rights are trumped, or where the independence of the judiciary is tilted in favour of a muscular executive.

Up until some 15 years ago, we deluded ourselves to attract, seduce and "Europeanize" behemoths in search of a new identity such as Putin's Russia and Erdoğan's Turkey. After the umpteenth constitutional reform, referendum, blitz-war and shutdown of independent media, we find ourselves with a Czar and a Sultan, who consolidated autocratic models that in many respects mirror each other. The post-Wall Europe that was meant to open up and expand, finds itself with three empires centered in Brussels, Moscow and Istanbul.

Think about the melancholic Brazil, which up until a decade ago launched visionary policies such as *Bolsa Família*, that lifted millions of families out of extreme poverty by giving subsidies on one condition: that they would send their kids to school and to regular health check-ups. It is hard to imagine a more laudable way to invest public money than in youth's health and education. Yet, the current Bolsonaro administration has curtailed *Bolsa Família*,[8] next to eroding the rule of law and other institutions of this fledgling democracy.

Consider India, that proud bastion of freedom in the developing world. Seventy years since gaining independence, this quasi-continental giant has defied the conventional wisdom, which sees democracy failing to stick in low-income countries.[9] However, democratic institutions present worrying signs of erosion. Prime Minister Modi has tarnished the independence of the judiciary and the military's own tradition for arm's length distance from politics.[10] He has gradually dismantled the pluralist, inclusive character of Indian democracy with a string of sectarian policies bordering on Islamophobia. At one point in the last decade, the Indian parliament had a quarter of its members under investigation or facing criminal charges; in 83 cases, the charges involved murder.[11]

The most potent charge against liberal democracy has come from China, whose embrace of the free market 40 years ago has been as successful as its deliberate rebuttal of liberal values. The rise of "autocratic capitalism" has spawned a cottage industry of reflections on the future of human progress. Some westerners openly admire the effectiveness of Beijing's supposedly meritocratic executive; others see its gradual democratization as only a matter of time. Chinese political leaders, including its own former premier have spoken of the inevitability of democracy.[12] But reality has its ways of creeping in. In effect, since then-president Deng Xiao Ping inaugurated his "Southern tour" of reforms in 1979 – for some, a more consequential year in history than 1989 – the Chinese economic story has constituted the 800 pound gorilla on the beaten path of Western modernity.[13] China's economic prowess is the living proof that autocracies can guarantee security and development at the same time.

In doing so, Beijing has upended the logic underpinning the liberal world order, namely that economic liberalization is followed by a political one. Whether or not Deng actually said that "to get rich is glorious", the Chinese Communist Party reinvented itself and guaranteed its own survival by lifting hundreds of millions of people out of extreme poverty. The world community may be appalled by the trumping of human rights in Hong Kong, but seen from Beijing, security and prosperity trump liberty anytime.

Political scientist Jeffrey Kopstein characterized the complexity inherent in this contradiction in an effective, if deliberately simplified way. When you promote liberal democracy, you can do it from below or from above. The interpretation of the events that led to the fall of the Berlin Wall and collapse of the communist regimes in 1989–91 offers an accurate rendering of this dynamic. Promoting democracy bottom-up is about "letting the course of freedom play itself out".[14] Accordingly, the emergence of democracy is the sheer result of people's power and civil society overthrowing tyrants. The most powerful instrument of this force is the ballot box. Promoting democracy top-down means looking at revolutions with uneasiness, worrying about their consequences and particularly about the less charming work of establishing checks and balances and planning reforms. In the case of the Velvet revolutions of the late-1980s, says Kopstein, "the true *dramatis personae*" of history were in the Kremlin. It was Mikhail Gorbachev, his attempt at transparency and reform, that more or less wittingly, tore down the Wall.

Plainly, in order to build and sustain democratic governance, you need both forces. The appeal of liberal democracy originates precisely from the combination of that most inalienable of rights, the vote, with the fundamental institutions of government: such as division of powers, protection of minorities and fundamental freedoms. This is what Fareed Zakaria, the journalist, calls: "constitutional liberalism", which at first might appear as a formulation needed to define the procedures of government, but it is really about its ultimate goals: preserving individual liberties within the rule of law. When seen in this light, "the 'Western model' is best symbolized not by the mass plebiscite but by the impartial judge".[15]

Democratic governance, in this respect, is akin to what military strategists call the pincer movement. The bottom-up forces that help topple tyrants have to be tempered, balanced and complemented by the top-down, elite-driven ones that shape and adapt institutions. The essence of constitutional liberalism, in this regard, is about locating the sources of power and finding a workable balance between its limitation and its accumulation. Increasingly *en vogue* in these illiberal times, calls for direct democracy appeal to the accumulation of power by citizens, potentially leading what Tocqueville called the "tyranny of the majority". Executives elected under this banner are inherently prone to the temptation to further usurp power, precisely because they claim to speak in the name of the people. For a workable, democratic governance, the twin, contradictory challenge is to extend and expand popular deliberation as much as possible, while taming popular passions as much as necessary. That is one feat that Nordic countries have managed to accomplish, in ways and with instruments that are or should be familiar to us all.

Epistocracy for the people

Alexander Hamilton, one of the United States' founding fathers, called them "imperial arbiters": individuals who have the role to protect the common interest, avoiding the special ones that pollute even the best intentions. Some two hundred years later, Francis Fukuyama added provocatively that: "good governance is a kind of aristocratic phenomenon".[16] But the point still stands: heirs to the British gentry of the sixteenth and seventeenth centuries, elites are the nobility that get their hands dirty in public life. They have time on their side and keep themselves aloof from the passions of democratic life. In this way, to paraphrase Italian statesman Alcide De Gasperi, they can afford to think about the next generations, rather than having to worry about the next election.

Before I am blamed of shameless elitism, I should hurry to refer to another founding father, Thomas Jefferson, who helpfully qualified that statement: "I agree with you that there is a natural aristocracy among men", he wrote, "the grounds of this are virtue and talents ... There is also an artificial aristocracy, founded on wealth and birth ... The natural aristocracy I consider as the most precious gift of nature, for the instruction the trusts and government of society ... May we not even say that the form of government is the best, which provides most effectually for a pure selection of these natural aristoi in the offices of government".[17]

Unwittingly, the Nordic governance experience has perfected this approach. As in other representative democracies, the social contract in Northern Europe is based on people delegating authority. Yet, some of the groups holding this authority are shielded from the distortions of democracy. The legitimacy of these *natural aristoi* relies not on the ballot box but on their competence and expertise. Welcome to epistocracy, the rule of those who know.

Existing definitions of epistocracy do come with more than a whiff of elitism. Jason Brennan translated it into a proposal whereby individual votes of politically informed citizens should count more. Bryan Caplan takes issue with the irrational beliefs and biases of ordinary voters.[18] Garett Jones argues that a mere "10% less democracy" would improve the outcomes of rich-world democracies.[19] Nordics have taken the epistocratic assumption to a radically "democratic" extreme, turning the *acquisition* of knowledge into the hallmark of their approach to governance.

At the roots of the Nordic epistocratic ethos, there is something quirky and innate, which at that latitude is known as the "law of Jante". This hails back to the story of a fictional town invented in 1933 by the Danish-Norwegian novelist Aksel Sandemose. That imaginary town, Jante, codified the rules inspired by civility, moderation, and respect that define the Nordic ethos. Sandemose describes, in a satirical vein, a model of social conduct according to which successes can only be reached by a collectivity and any individualism is regarded with suspicion. The most important of Jante's rules is "don't think that you are more special than others or that you are better than us". To this day, the Jante law is referred to in Scandinavia almost always in pejorative terms, as something that suppresses creativity and suffocates individual initiative. When I wrote about the "law" for an American magazine, the Swedish singer-songwriter Maria Marcus explained that the Jante law is "99% negative".[20]

Yet, the Jante law takes a radical and forceful position on the fundamental question of epistocratic rule: the access to knowledge. The stellar reputation of the Nordic education systems traces back to it. Its more innovative features have become the stuff of urban mythology: no grades until middle school, no rote-learning, prioritizing pupils' ability to play outdoors. It would be impossible to fully understand this system without appreciating the solidaristic mindset that underpins it. At the micro level, it could be about finding least common denominators among pupils and their learning paces. At the macro one, as the Nordic ministers of education wrote in a joint communique, students have to become "creators of a democratic and sustainable society, in social, cultural, environmental and economic terms".[21]

To counter the negative association with the Jante law, these are also the very qualities that, according to Harvard education expert Tony Wagner, enable Nordic education systems to make pupils "innovation ready". It is thanks to this readiness that small and nimble Nordic nations excel in anything from software innovation to, indeed, music. Specialized music education imparted in Sweden since primary school must at least partly be responsible for class acts for every generation, from ABBA, to Roxette, to Avicii. Perhaps it is they who are the real Swedish royalty.

Some American economists retort disdainfully that Scandinavia is fraught with "cuddly capitalism",[22] a hybrid model where the state intervenes and meddles with private initiative. Cuddly capitalism, they argue, could not survive without the protection and baseline investments of the United States and Europe. This may well be true, but it does not take away that the Scandinavian state is the most far-sighted of entrepreneurs: it takes the responsibility to educate citizens and protects them from failures, with the understanding that, if they succeed, the shareholders are the whole nation. As the Finnish investment agency SITRA put it, innovation enables the long-term refinancing of the welfare state.[23]

That leads to what is arguably the most important quality of Nordic education: it is a life-long project. In Denmark, for one, since the beginning of the last century, the system of free schools for children was accompanied by adult education, the "people's high schools", pioneered by nineteenth-century Danish pastor and educator Nicolaj Grundvig. In the words of Bo Lidegaard, the Danish historian we met in the first chapter: "There was a deep understanding that in order to really take power, people needed more knowledge, more education and a different form of knowledge and education to become independent, democratic citizens". At a time when universal suffrage was still an illusion, it was education that liberated people: "It paved the way to real democracy" continues Lidegaard "by enabling people to become mature by way of knowledge and the self-respect that made it possible for them to take power". This is the secret of the Nordic epistocratic rule.

One emblematic application in which this life-long and egalitarian approach to knowledge manifests itself is in the role of experts in public life. Much like we should do when consulting the family doctor instead of searching Google for miraculous remedies, a visceral belief in the power of education is expressed as confidence in expertise in informing decision making. Incidentally, we used to expect the same from a bank's financial advisors when taking on a mortgage, a point that led Peter Murray of Harvard Law School to suggest that the independent, French-style notary would have come a long way in tempering the excesses and fraud that led to the 2007 subprime mortgage crisis in the United States.[24]

A textbook example of this faith in expertise is parliamentary-mandated commissions. In some Western countries, the creation of expert commissions often turn out to represent an expedient to bypass complex, sensitive subjects or taking unpopular decisions. In well-governed countries, the premise for the creation of such commissions is that the thornier problems have to be lifted from the political arena and brought to the table of experts, whether they come from academia, civil society, business or civil service (full disclosure: the institute I worked for in Denmark is regularly tasked to join or contribute to such commissions).

Europe's North may be a paragon of this, but it is not an exception. The *New Yorker*'s George Packer, for example, recalls with a touch of nostalgia the American experience of the 1950s and 1960s, characterized by bipartisan fora and individuals "in politics, business, and the media that could hold the center together".[25] He mentions the case of the 1964 National Commission on Technology, Automation and Economic Progress created by President Lyndon Johnson and made up of labour, corporate leaders and civil rights activists alike. The Commission's key recommendations included minimum wage and job-training programmes, the kind of themes debated in Northern European social-democracies. It may be just a curious coincidence that a couple of years before Johnson's Commission was constituted, the head of the Swedish Federation of Labour, and the head of the Employers' Federation, had been travelling *together* on a tour across the United States to spread the gospel of the Swedish model.[26] But it is certainly no accident that President Johnson's tenure is associated with the notion of the Great Society, which heralded the largest welfare expansion in America's history.[27]

Up until that period, lawyers, notaries, journalists and professors held respectable roles in society precisely because of their knowledge and their commitment to use it wisely and impartially. They would give advice and opinions based on a genuinely non-partisan, rigorous view of public service. Titans of industry would associate their names with organizations that could uphold rigour and integrity, such as the Brookings Institution or the Carnegie Endowment. Institutions such as the US Supreme Court or the Federal Reserve are respected also because their pronouncements and measures are not immediately influenced by political considerations or public opinion. Zakaria compares these individuals and institutions to those first-class male passengers on the *Titanic* who refused to board rescue ships in order to save women and children first.

This kind of civic virtue and sense of duty, even when leading to the sacrifice of one's life, was something that was expected from the elites.[28] As for the culture of compromise, even Ronald Reagan, that most ideological of US presidents, "talked in black and white" but "governed in grey" and was fond of telling his advisers: "I'd rather get 80 percent of what I want than go over a cliff with my flag flying".[29]

Unsurprisingly, this mindset is sorely missing in today's polarized political environment. Governments and parliaments receive plenty of advice from foundations, think-tanks, and the media, who sell their expertise to produce partisan views. As commentator Clive Crook lamented in relation to the United States: "The curse of U.S. politics is not just that it's polarized but also that there's so damned much of it. Unaligned expert opinion is hard to find. Unaligned commentators are even rarer. Top jobs in the civil service, several layers down into the bureaucracy, are given to political appointees. Experts brought into government for specific projects are required to be Democrats or Republicans first, and experts second: They become another species of politician".[30] Just like CEOs awarding themselves hefty bonuses before quitting or being fired, in the midst of a shipwreck, elites try to save themselves first because they have the means to do it.

Scandinavia is not immune from the marketization of public life. The award-winning Danish TV series *Borgen*, narrating the public and domestic tribulations of a fictional woman head of government, Prime Minister Birgitte Nyborg, gives away the intimate confession: "We all have a right to a new car and a smashing new kitchen, a big family, a mistress, and a yacht. We live in a world where we are busy to pursue our happiness ... The Danish people would give everything for solidarity. They are always ready to make sacrifices. But we have forgotten it".[31]

It is a screenshot of the Western condition: cheap loans and ubiquitous technology tempt citizens in the High North as anywhere else. Before Covid-19 hit, the stadium of the national football team in Copenhagen hosted the final round of *X-Factor*, which glues half of the population in front of a screen. In the wake of the financial crisis, the whole region was hit by real-estate bubbles and financial speculations under the nose of politicians, paradoxically even in some of those semi-public cooperatives described by Marquis Childs as the futuristic example of wealth redistribution.

Even so, this race towards the bottom of instant gratification has not tarnished the respect for elites in Scandinavia. As we have seen, citizens are raised, trained and educated to respect the institutions of democracy. As a result, they do not resent experts or their ultra-rich, and they have a few, and this respect is mutual. It is not about being part of the elite or being against it: Mr Rasmussen could be a captain of industry or a construction worker, as long as all the Rasmussens belong to the same tribe. As we shall see, tribalism comes with a dark side, for the many who in a multicultural society are not part of the tribe. But in the relationship between elites and citizens, these ties remain the bedrock of good governance. Dialogue is a permanently open platform and never taken for granted. It is, in fact, a little miracle that is nurtured, celebrated and repeated every summer in many of the Nordic countries.

The conversation

The idea originally occurred to Olof Palme, later to become a prime minister of Sweden, towards the end of the 1970s. He loved to spend the summer holidays with his family on the island of Gotland, about an hour's flight away from Stockholm, where, while he was still minister of education, he started to improvise some rallies; in the first one, he jumped on the back of a truck and spoke to 200 bystanders. Thanks to the charisma and popularity of the social-democratic statesman, the event took off. In the 1980s, when Palme was prime minister, the meeting saw the participation of all of Sweden's political and economic leaders. *Almedalsveckan*, the week of Almedal, named after the central park on Gotland where it takes place, has become a veritable festival of governance. Without flags, or rather with all of them, it is inclusive of parties, unions, media, and thousands of private citizens, who care to discuss the most important questions shaping their society.

The festival almost stopped after Palme's brutal murder in 1986. His widow, who herself barely escaped death in the assassination plot, persuaded the new prime minister to continue it. In the last decade, *Almedalsveckan* has smashed every record of participation, with an average of 1,800 organizations represented and 3,800 debates of all kinds organized over the course of the week. Gradually, several other Nordic countries, Finland, Norway, Denmark and even Estonia have created their own versions of *Almedalsveckan*, at the beginning of summer, and possibly on an island, away from chancelleries and television studios.

One might object that many other countries have historic political festivals, often in summertime, but even the organizers of these events would agree that in most cases they are promoted by a party, a faction, if not destined to divide at least hoping to promote some partisan views. To give just one example, the "Festival of Unity", which is the largest of such gatherings held in Italy every summer, is named after a newspaper (*l'Unità*) that no longer exists, and was founded by the early-twentieth-century communist philosopher and leader

Antonio Gramsci. The second largest one is organized by Communion and Liberation, a conservative Catholic outfit. You get the gist.

There is something fundamentally different about the Nordic festivals, which over the years have attracted the admiration and pilgrimage of delegates from every corner of the world. These events are unique in their being intensely political while not being partisan and for the declared mission to renew the relationship between the people and the elites by means of dialogue. This formula finds a conceptual justification in the thinking of Danish theologist Hal Koch. Writing at the end of the Second World War, Koch explained that democracy was to be found in conversation. Without constitutionally protected rights, he conceded, democracy would have far more serious problems. But once we ascertain that all people have equal rights, democracy must find its middle way by means of interlocution: "It is conversation (dialogue) and mutual understanding and respect that is the essence of democracy".[32]

Nordic democracy is thus a dialogue, at once passionate and quiet. That is not an oxymoron. Any foreigner witnessing a conversation among Nordics might have noticed these qualities, the long pauses and the surreal silences. Disagreements are ironed out by listening without rolling eyes, nodding without lifting brows. That some might get a little impatient in following the rhythms of these conversations is perhaps not surprising. Michel Foucault also wrote of this after his unhappy stint in Uppsala: "It is perhaps the mutism of the Swedes, their silence and their habit of talking with elliptical sobriety, which prompted me to start speaking [writing?] and develop this endless chatter that I believe can only irritate a

Swede".[33] Susan Sontag concurred: "Silence is the Swedish national vice. Will you laugh if I invoke Greta Garbo? Honestly, Sweden is full of prosaic, graceless mini-Garbos".[34]

The metaphor of the silent film is unfair and, in retrospect, shortsighted. Today we all live in noisy societies. We have elevated social media to the level of personal, unfiltered megaphones. We communicate in ever faster and more fragmented ways, in what have become mere echo-chambers, a myriad of restricted or closed groups in which different ideas get systematically stigmatized. Talk shows are arenas where slogans are repeated ad nauseam in a cacophony of onedirectional proclaims. It is hard to present the Nordic conversation better than Dennis Kucinich, a one-time candidate for the US presidency, after a pilgrimage to *Almedalsveckan*:

When you see the kind of internecine conflict that happens in the United States – the partisan divide, the dichotomous thinking, the separation from each other – there is a different thing happening here in Sweden at Almedalen, which is a sense of a common bond as citizens with a common purpose for the nation. [...] I've had a chance to meet people from every level of society, decision makers as well as citizens, and there's a sense that things matter in these kind of discussions, which are direct, relatively low-key, nonconfrontational, matter-of-fact. And behind it is – what animates it is a sense of commitment to each other and to the nation.[35]

Something that Kucinich underplays is the accessibility of the elites. Lao Tzu, the founder of Taoism, wrote that "the best leader is the one that people barely know he exists". It is unusual to meet the prime minister of a country on a ferry boat, with his daughters and two Labradors, conversing casually with some sleepy truck-drivers, a scene that presented itself to me in Denmark. In the same way, there is something perverse in the idolatry associated with new upcoming leaders in some countries, especially if those leaders are young and charismatic. To hope is all well and good, but it should never subside to an abdication of responsibility. Citizens in a mature democracy not only have the right but the responsibility to enter into a dialogue with their leaders, and the appropriate channels have to exist for this dialogue to take place.

The social contract in Europe's North is so tight because it binds citizens and the state, both ways. While every country has its constitution, the social contract is based on practices, usages and above all trust, embodying the spirit of a nation. To put it bluntly, if citizens regarded tax evasion as some form of resistance against a corrupt or inefficient state, the social contract could not realistically foresee improvements in healthcare or education. Worse still, it becomes a sorry tale of mutual recriminations and unmet expectations. When in countries like Romania, the independent anti-corruption agency is the country's most popular institution, the underlying assumption is that the social contract is irreparably torn.[36]

In this respect, Scandinavia may be futuristic, but it is not a Utopia. As noted, a side-effect of a tight social contract based on trust and unwritten rules is conformism, in so far as it often becomes very difficult to incorporate sensibilities from outside the mainstream. Therefore, it is not accidental that the arrival of right-wing or nativist sentiments in these lands preceded their arrival in the rest of Europe and the West.

It is a symptom that the Nordic "conversation" has radically changed over the past two decades.

Year after year, statistics bear out the stereotype that the Nordic countries are the most highly-taxed in the world.[37] Nordics are the prototypes of a state engaging energetically in the functioning of the market, in the ways masterfully described by Childs. Yet, not unlike other Western countries since the Reagan-Thatcher revolution of the 1980s, the opposite has happened in the past half-century: the market has gradually but ever more pervasively entered into the functioning of the state. The retrenchment of the state has affected the Nordic region just like any other advanced democracy. In Sweden, for example, that bastion of social democracy made up of free education and universal healthcare, public spending as a percentage of GDP has declined by a quarter in the last two decades. As we shall see in the next chapter, subcontracting public services to the private sector, whether in the form of school vouchers, healthcare provision or labour market policies, has become routine.[38]

The people's mindset has changed accordingly: Nordic bookstores are said to register a growing interest for libertarian authors such as Milton Friedman and Ayn Rand, the same who had referred to the welfare state as "the most evil national psychology ever described".[39] In the 1990s a young and ambitious Danish politician by the name of Anders Fogh Rasmussen, published a manifesto tellingly entitled, *From the Social State to the Minimal State*, in which, among other things, he preached the necessity of privatizations because, "the free market determines the size of the rewards. Market rewards are not right or wrong, fair or unfair. They are just a fact".[40] Fogh Rasmussen became prime minister for a decade at the beginning of this century and practiced this logic – so stridently different from the Nordic welfare state – in effective and sometimes brutal ways.

This radical turn to the right did not limit itself to economic values but extended also to political ones. A landmark case for this was the crisis that erupted in the wake of the publication of cartoons depicting the Prophet Mohammed in the Danish daily *JyllandsPosten* in 2005. The most mind-boggling aspect of that story was not the 11 representations of the Prophet, offensive mostly for their rudeness, nor even the assassination attempts on the cartoonist and the editor of the paper. The tipping point of that crisis occurred when Fogh Rasmussen, then prime minister, refused to meet the ambassadors of the Islamic countries who had asked for a clarifying meeting. The refusal was motivated exclusively by the principle of freedom of expression, which prevented the Danish government not only from censoring the newspaper, but also apparently from engaging in any form of dialogue with foreign countries.

As much as the cartoons, it was Fogh Rasmussen's radical interpretation that caused protests, boycotts, casualties all over the world, and placed Copenhagen once and for all on the map of Islamist terrorism. Freedom of expression is a sacred principle of liberal democracy, but the rigid stance of Rasmussen was a choice that took precedence over other imperatives, such as for example that of preserving the safety and security of one's citizens.

In the same way the Nordics anticipated progressive experiments and trends, they also anticipated a nativist, populist backlash against immigration and globalization that the whole Western world has since experienced. Right-wing populist movements in the Nordic countries – their origins, policy platforms and popular support – are very different. In the Norwegian case, they have a pronounced neoliberal streak, while in Sweden they have a dark association with their neo-Nazi past. In Norway and Finland, they have participated in governing coalitions, and mellowed as a result of the thrust-and-parry that government requires. In Denmark, right-wing populists have typically supported minority governments from the outside. "Almost none of the parties", says political scientist Cas Mudde, "is a really good, perfect fit for what we see as the prototype" of a populist party.[41]

The common denominator in all of them is that in the past two decades right-wing populism has passed from being fringe movements to occupying the centre of the political debate. On questions like immigration or indeed the place of Islam in western societies, their positions have become mainstream. The traditional centre-left and centre-right parties, often in freefall like in the rest of Europe, could not but accept compromises or copycat some of their positions, as did the Danish Social Democrats, who regained power in 2019 on a deliberately anti-immigrant platform. In Sweden, populists are still shunned by traditional parties, but the once taboo looks increasingly untenable as the Sweden Democrats, as the far-right party there is called, continue to grow in popularity while centrists shrink.

The Nordic social contract was not dismantled by the emergence of right-wing populism. Yet, it tightened and retrenched, harking back to tribal instincts to the point of sleepwalking into mindless intolerance. The culture of conversation underpinning it has morphed dramatically in order to accommodate far-right instances. To phrase it in the way mainstream Scandinavia would put it, right-wing populists have gradually been granted the "right to formulate problems".

That is why those island summer festivals are so paradigmatic of the Nordic middle way of governance. They incarnate participation, commitment and passion in the conversation between elites and citizens. They also symbolize that consensus is achieved through deliberation and socialization. This conversation does not need to be mediated by an outside arbiter, but it does require common sense and good will. Not coincidentally, then, in recent years some of the most intense conversations have concerned issues brought forward by far-right parties, the extent to which these can or should indeed be mainstreamed, what they say about the ways in which these nations have changed as a result.

As the popular Queen of Denmark Margrethe II said in a New Year's speech a few years ago: "Mutual respect is best achieved when one also knows what all parties stand for. Only here can real conversation begin. But it is important that it becomes a conversation: to talk together, to listen to the other party, so that there are no two monologues between deaf people, where everyone holds their own and does not understand what the other has to say, because one thinks to know it in advance".[42]

3

The crystal curtain: a culture of governance

"I actually feel pretty comfortable in New York. I get scared, like, in Sweden". Lou Reed, the frontman of the Velvet Underground is thinking aloud while playing himself as the dishevelled city-dweller in the movie *Blue in the Face:* "It's kind of empty, they're all drunk, everything works. If you stop at a traffic light and don't turn your engine off, people come over and talk to you about it. You go to the medicine cabinet and open it up and there will be a little poster saying: 'In case of suicide, call ...'. You turn on the TV, there's an ear operation. These things scare me. New York? No."[1]

I would not know if the show on otolaryngology ever took place. To make up for it, there has been another, on the first channel of the Norwegian state television, which showed logs burning in a fireplace for 12 straight hours. The debate in the television studio centred on issues such as chopping, stacking and the best music to accompany the log burning operation ("nerdy" items, by the producer's own admission).[2]

The point, so bizarrely illustrated by Lou Reed, is that the Nordics are different, in ways that are so perfect as to seem to some extent inhuman. Authors Henrik Berggren and Lars Trägårdh even wrote a book asking the somewhat disturbing question: "Are the Swedes humans?"[3] As a "Southerner" living in these lands, I have often been tempted to associate the Nordics' sophistication, disarming simplicity, precision and ruthless pragmatism, to übermenschian qualities. In this, Nordic societies remind me of an operating room or a chemistry lab: everything is pristine, sanitized, shiny, stainless steel. Bespectacled scientists in their immaculate white overcoats are free to experiment on humanity's next frontier.

Theoretically, a united Europe was supposed to attenuate these differences. For sure in the North they will continue to consume beer and butter, while in the South we reclaim the superiority of wine and olive oil. In the disorganized South, improvization is a necessity that becomes a virtue. Mistrust is a trait that is almost somatized in the way we obliquely look at each other. Yet, for the vast majority of the two million Europeans that constitute the Erasmus generation, Europe is a mindset and a way of life. The opening of borders and the common currency are epochal achievements. They have reinforced a narrative and a socialization that has brought Europeans together, if not in what a united Europe might look like, at least in a basic understanding of the challenges and opportunities that the future might hold.

As the veteran British diplomat Robert Cooper put it in his essential book *The Breaking of Nations*: "When you have a problem you cannot solve, enlarge the context".[4] Time and again in the past, Europe succeeded in reverting inward-looking navel-gazing and impasses by bringing in new resources and new thinking from the outside. The fall of the Berlin Wall was the pivotal moment in this respect. The key intuition being that security and stability could be best attained not by means of erecting barriers but by means of exchanges and integration. The accession of ten new former-communist states of Central Europe into the European Union in 2004 was the zenith of this moment.

In retrospect, however, those 15 extraordinary years between 1989 and 2004 should be seen as an exception, rather than as a stage on the unstoppable march towards a new European century.[5] The three historic achievements of those years – the enlargement towards the East, the common currency and the free movement of people – have all come under severe pressure. Europe spent 70 years building a sophisticated borderless space but it has taken this miraculous achievement for granted and the tables have now turned. The Covid-19 pandemic shook our convictions in a matter of days. All of a sudden, curfews, border closures and travel bans were not a distant memory from our forefathers but a daily necessity. Survival equalled not openness and exchanges but total lockdown and closure.

When seen in this light, the pandemic was not an isolated occurrence but came to culminate, accelerate and sanction a number of man-made trends that had preceded it. Before Covid-19 hit, new Central European member states such as Hungary and Poland had disavowed their democratic achievements. In a matter of a few years, they reverted to an illiberal path where courts are politicized, the press is muzzled, parliaments are subjugated to an all-powerful government, with echoes uncannily similar to their communist past. Before that, Europe's belief in solidarity, humanism and multicultural openness had fatally crumbled during the refugee crisis of 2015. In a domino effect of unilateral national decisions, country after country followed its neighbour in closing borders and rejecting boatloads of destitute victims of tyranny and oppression.

But in the beginning, before the refugee crisis, before the Central European reversal and before Covid-19, what shattered the European dream and laid bare the fair-weathered assumptions of its integration process was the financial crisis of 2008. The EU's sovereign-debt and banking crises revealed glaring and underestimated gaps between the Northern parts of Europe and the countries in the South. In doing so, it woke up the ghosts of prejudice, division, disintegration that had defined the chequered history of Europe's twentieth century. Europe tore down the Iron Curtain, only to erect a new one, invisible but incredibly sturdy, which one might term the Crystal Curtain.

This chapter aims to shed light on this new crystal curtain, to enable us to see the reflections and to warn us not to walk into it. It tackles the slippery question of the role of culture in European governance practices, first by offering a brief historical excursus into some of the signposts that have shaped our perceptions. I then actualize these cultural fault-lines in today's Europe and argue that European policy making has either wilfully ignored or culpably exaggerated cultural factors. I conclude explaining why and how, to our peril, Europe has never properly accounted for the role that these factors play in policy formation and political compromises.

I would have loved Martin Luther

Possible explanations for the division between Europe's North and South are many and range from social trust and tax collection, to labour-market legislation and competitiveness. For years, Southern governments would repeatedly plead with the North for greater solidarity, in recognition of design flaws of the single currency and balance-of-payments disequilibria in the eurozone. Northern countries, on the other hand, stressed their inability to take on more liability for debts incurred by nations they had learned to mistrust.[6] "Over the years", writes political economist Matthias Matthijs, "there was a gradual widening of the popular-perception gap separating a 'financially more orthodox' northern core of surplus countries that mainly saved, invested, produced and exported, from a 'debt-ridden' Southern periphery of deficit countries that predominantly borrowed, consumed, and imported".[7]

Underpinning this narrative, however, there is another kind of dualism. Not between North and South, or creditors and debtors. It is between, on the one hand, the pursuit of homogenizing and amalgamating cultures, specifically through the formulation, implementation and enforcement of common rules, standards and schemes. On the other hand, there is continued and inherent differentiation, particularly in political cultures, understood as the set of society's values and beliefs and their influence on institutions.

The tension between cultural amalgamation and standardization on the one hand and cultural differentiation and distinction on the other has accompanied European history, pervaded its public discourse. It has impinged on social and political practices and, more recently, on the overall effectiveness of mechanisms put in place to manage our interactions. The continent's enduring tensions between North and South offer a particularly useful window to explain why the same rules, approaches and policies have produced different outcomes in different European countries. At the root of this dissonance between desired results and reality is the role of culture, understood as the complex range of political mind-sets and nation-specific social habits, in the evolution of Europe's governance.

The two mindsets are diametrically opposed, even in their conceptual inspiration. The idea of standardization and amalgamation stems from the hypothesis that rule-making and rule implementation are a direct consequence of rational choices. Accordingly, governments' action may be inspired by different criteria and preferences, but it is ultimately the result of economic rationality: if you do not respect, say, the Stability and Growth Pact on the EU monetary union, a government has to raise taxes and that is against its own interest. Progress towards better governance is therefore purely logical; cultural variations are seen as ultimately secondary. In an old pamphlet about the lessons from the Swedish socio-economic model, entitled "How bright are the Northern Stars?", US scholar Mancur Olson, one of the most prominent proponents of the virtues of *Homo economicus*, puts this bluntly: "Every culture and every people have some obviously distinctive characteristics ... but after sustained examination these claims usually turn out to be pseudo-explanations".[8]

A diametrically opposite proposition accords culture a central place in the formation and evolution of the processes of governing. This may lead to gradual processes of socialization. But at its heart it posits that the historical experiences, language and religion of a people are constant and influence their political and economic institutions. There is a vast literature that underpins this thesis. It traces back to the origins of "cultural economics" that since the time of Thomas Malthus and David Ricardo over 200 years ago sought to pin down cultural factors in the formation of wealth and prosperity. What turned out to be the climax was offered by Max Weber's thesis about the role of Protestant ethics in the formation of capitalist prosperity.[9]

Perhaps because of the over-simplifications that stuck with the Weberian hypothesis, the cultural argument in institutional analysis gradually lost steam. Yet it was resurrected over time and is now experiencing an intellectual revival. Putnam's argument about social capital in central Italy as opposed to the South, expounded in the previous chapter, could at its heart be viewed as a work of cultural economics applied to institutional analysis. A popular strand of institutionalists, championed by Daron Acemoglu and James Robinson and their celebrated *Why Nations Fail*, has followed. Their merit, other than popularizing a number of highly interesting case studies from all over the world, has been to put the role of culture in context. They qualify culture's role and factor in criteria such as resources and even randomness in the formation of prosperity.[10]

In Europe itself, this argument has an even longer pedigree. When you coalesce space and time – and you are a social scientist rather than a theoretical physicist – you end up with fascinating ethnographic explorations. Here history and geography have become engrained in our understanding as Europeans. One of the seminal works of this genre is Eric Jones' *The European Miracle*.[11] This is a systematic attempt to trace Europe's political and economic development across history as a product of its geography. As he puts it: "Europe did not spend the gifts of its environment 'as rapidly as it got them in a mere insensate multiplication of the common life'. This phrase from H. G. Wells (in *Men like Gods*) sums up the quality of Europeanness". Europeans, posits Jones, got lucky with their geography: mountains and rivers created natural boundaries. In time, these boundaries delimited polities, their size, and their specificities: principates, semi-imperial units, and proto-national states. Europeans used geography to their advantage since the Middle Ages to grow their population on the basis of the territory available to them.

Thanks to his enthusiastic admiration of the European case, Jones' thesis has gained a great following since it was first published, but it has also attracted much opposition. In effect, it has been the European equivalent of Bernard Lewis' provocative essay *What Went Wrong?*, which posited the inherent clash between Islamic culture and modernity.[12] In Jones' case, factoring in geography and the natural environment in this way smacks of culturalist exceptionalism and has been predictably accused of Eurocentrism. Moreover, this rather deterministic approach seems to ignore the contribution of man-made events, whether the Enlightenment or the Industrial Revolution, in European development.[13]

As flawed as it may be, however, Jones' thesis is useful to introduce the ethnographic foundations of "othering" practices in Europe, and particularly those that relate to the North–South divide. Throughout Europe's centuries-long history, geographical markers have been used and abused *ad nauseam* to derive cultural and political specificities. Take the welfare state, which according to Jacques Derrida and Jürgen Habermas is, together with secularism and the rule of law, the most distinctive feature of Europe's modern development.[14] Danish political scientist Gert T. Svendsen traces it back to the Vikings; to the hard, bare, frozen terrain that they were forced to inhabit. Geography led the Vikings to shift from "roving to stationary banditry" around the tenth century, to survive and provide for their community.[15] This gives an almost mystical ethnographic explanation about why the welfare state has developed to such an extent in Northern Europe. Uffe Østergaard, a historian, traces the welfare state to the Lutheran Church's "universalist" practice of delivering public goods to the population (he cites a Danish church ordinance from 1539 stating that "children shall be taught properly [and] schools and the poor shall have their food").[16]

As partisan as Jones' thesis may sound, the idea of Europe and its evolution across history has revolved around this ethnographic contradiction. On the one hand, the long-term narrative of integration and unification, the "longue durée" of French historian Fernand Braudel, that would inexorably bring the Continent together in a multicultural, ecumenical embrace. On the other, the inherent, invisible differences between regions, which have never quite succeeded in reconciling Europe's cultures and have resurfaced time and again across history.

Consider ancient Rome, that unprecedented experiment of cultural assimilation. The greatness of the Roman Empire is typically associated with the relative integration that it brought about. To this day, one can only be awestruck by the ruins of ancient streets, amphitheatres and aqueducts from North Africa to Germany and realize the scale and the ambition of the Roman experiment to bring closer far away geographies. This ambition extended beyond architecture and infrastructure to areas such as citizenship, public administration, the military and the rule of law. And yet this confident tale of imperial assimilation is constantly dotted with clear-eyed admonitions of its limitations. The Roman historian Tacitus, in his *Germania*, was among the first to observe the political health of Northern Europe, their meritocratic system of public office, common political deliberations, and the more inclusive role of women. Julius Caesar reached similar conclusions in his *De Bello Gallico*, where the Rhine, the mighty river cutting across continental Europe, is as much a political and defensive line, as it is a cultural boundary between Roman civilization and Germanic peoples.[17]

The subsequent era, the Middle Ages, displayed a similar puzzling contradiction. On the one hand, as Eric Jones suggests in *The European Miracle*, this was the era when the territorial peculiarities and advantages of the European land matched with a relative increase in temperatures and deforestation, produced an increase in arable land. The very term "Christendom" relates to how religion formed a common governance platform created by the Church and unified by the usage of Latin, corroborating the impression of a period of cultural amalgamation. Historians such as George Duby and Jacques Le Goff have gone to great lengths to codify the peculiarities of "medieval man", their mental structures organized around symbols, emblems and flags and the organization of society around priests, warriors and economic producers.[18]

At the same time, as we shall see in Chapter 5, the Middle Ages are typically referred to as the era of fragmentation *par excellence*, the quintessential symbol of a past of fractures, ruptures and disorder. It was, in the words of historian Niall Ferguson, an era "of waning empires and religious fanaticism; of endemic plunder and pillage in the world's forgotten regions; of economic stagnation and civilization's retreat into a few fortified enclaves".[19]

In the European imagination, this tale of cultural division culminates with the Renaissance, a thesis immortalized by the Weberian hypothesis on the Protestant ethics of capitalism. This is a story where culture does play a crucial and fascinating role, and which has unwittingly come to crystallize in governance practices. The Reformation occupies a central place in a narrative of European division: there was something rotten in Rome and the North felt (or rather "protested") the need for reform. But how much of this reading is really applicable to Martin Luther and his momentous decision, now just over half millennium ago, to affix his 95 theses to the gate of Wittenberg castle?[20]

Initially, Luther felt compelled to act in the name of the whole of Christianity: he was an Augustinian monk who wanted to reform what existed, not create a new Church. The abuse of indulgences – payment to the Church as penance for sins committed – brought about alienation and represented an extreme exploitation of a typical Southern trait: the need for intermediaries. The Saints, the Virgin Mary, and above all the clergy represented obligatory channels between God and believers. The sacrament of Confession is emblematic of an institution that was founded on the intermediation of a body of professionals of the Faith. Combined with emerging differences regarding economic development, this need for intermediaries exacerbated the distance of a culture, the Northern European one, which privileged local cohesion, autonomy and self-reliance. In such context, indulgences represent a microcosm of distorted practices of governance: communities inspired by civic discipline and participation need to relate to an authority, which is far away and communicates mostly orally, at a time when plainly, words do not match deeds.

A long series of encounters and confrontations followed. In 1518, a frontal clash took place between the Church and

Luther the heretic. In the following years, the disagreements shifted on the necessity of the Church to practice the Confession. Catholics and Lutherans started to look for compromises on anything from free will to methods of penance. The discussions on the need to eliminate the Mass, for example, reveal profound cultural differences: between the ostentation of the Roman liturgy, which theatrically divides the world between actors and spectators, and the more integrated and egalitarian Germanic experience. The reading of diplomatic dispatches reveals clearly that there were several moments in which trust among the parties could have brought about an agreement and avoid a schism. But when the negotiation moved from the theological aspects to the political ones, Protestants and Catholics gave up trying to find agreement.

What is often overlooked is that the instances that brought about the Reformation were not entirely foreign to Southern sensibilities. In his diplomatic dispatches, Niccolò Machiavelli praised the Germanic confederation as an example of political "*virtù*". Similarly in his *Memories*, Florentine philosopher Francesco Guicciardini comes as far as recognizing that if it wasn't for his employment with the Papal States, he would have followed Martin Luther. It is worth reporting his reasoning in full:

Nevertheless the important roles that I have had for several popes imposed me to love their greatness for my own special interest; it wasn't for this, *I would have loved Martin Luther like myself*, not in order to free myself of the rules of the Christian religion in the way this is interpreted and commonly understood, but to punish this bunch of fools in the proper way, which is to say to leave them either without vices or without authority.[21]

From this point of view, and at the risk of contradicting Weber, the Reformation was not an exception or a turning point in European history. On the contrary, it represented the tip of an iceberg of something much deeper that had always existed, between those who sought to magnify cultural differences and those who tried to level them. We have seen that the very same doubts and distinctions were raised from the Roman times to the Middle Ages. A couple of centuries after the Reformation, the Enlightenment brought about further inputs for a universal "cultural peace", based on rationality, science and critical thinking. These are commons that to this day we rightly cherish as the bedrock of modernity. The Age of Light is the most natural precursor of today's knowledge society. Even so, in the decades that followed, the clashes between Prussian Lutheranism and conservative Catholicism, not for nothing known as *Kulturkampf*, cultural battle, resurfaced. Colonialism and Darwinism planted the seeds of cultural discrimination, which culminated with fascism and Nazism and brought national exceptionalism to catastrophic extremes.

Now: if this struggle between cultural integration and cultural distinction has crossed Europe's history for two thousand years, can we really be surprised that it has resurfaced, time and again, in today's European Union?

Meridionalism

It is perhaps an irony of history that in contemporary Europe itself, the birthplace of all the seminal work and events on the role of culture in economics, politics and institutions, the cultural factor is today so often banalized, exaggerated or ignored in policy making. The impression is that in European policy circles, the cultural factor is an afterthought, never quite taken seriously and weighed for the constant and yet perennially changing role it continues to play in European governance. Think of it this way: if you compare vast geographies, say in Asia or Africa, and factor in culture, governance differences are self-evident. That has given rise to serious analysis and, for policy makers, to complex and often intractable problems, from immigration to multicultural integration in our societies. It was the same in Europe until recently. Hailing from Greece or Italy and living as a *Gastarbeiter*, labour migrant, in Germany or Switzerland in the 1960s could have resulted in stark contrasts and discrimination, not unlike those that Pakistani or Bangladeshi migrants face in Western Europe today.

Yet, ever since European cooperation started to gain momentum in the 1950s, the political discourse has gradually side-lined this cultural factor. "United in Diversity" is the European mantra and slogan. But analysis and intellectual debate has been imbued by the same self-fulfilling prophecy that has accompanied European integration: cultures exist and diversity should be celebrated, as long as we also accept that they are gradually converging in an ecumenical European embrace. Accordingly, one does not need a visa to live and work in another European country; we do not need to change currency most of the time, we do not need to worry about our mobile company overcharging roaming costs.

As a result, cultural differences are filed as an afterthought in the realm of folklore – German orderliness, Dutch rudeness,

Italian flamboyance, Greek laziness. At most they are confined to which foods you bring to a dinner party and at what time you have dinner itself. Where there continue to be differences, they are stereotypical, brushed off with a laughter as factors that at best beautify and spice up Europe's diversity. Only when real disagreement occurs, whether because of a financial crisis or a pandemic, these tongue-in-cheek explanations come back with a vengeance and colour our judgement to the detriment of sound and reasonable analysis and conflict resolution.

These ebbs and flows in relation to the cultural factor in Europe continue to repeat themselves. There are powerful homogenizing forces at play (something which in Europe, we shall see, takes the name of "convergence"), often backed by large resources and stringent criteria. The Recovery and Resilience Fund, a groundbreaking programme approved by the EU in the wake of the Covid-19 pandemic, will distribute resources of €750 billion, in the forms of grants and loans to the countries most severely hit by the pandemic. The fund, probably the first European example of mutualization of debt, is in addition to a regular EU budget that already averages €1 trillion over seven years.

Such remarkable investments could not be achieved without a painstaking search for compromises, whether in the language formulating agreements or in the diplomacy needed to bring them about. Media and increasingly influential populist politicians complain alternatively about the near-autocratic imposition of European rules as much as about Europe's weakness. They conveniently ignore that all European positions, a European "will" on any given issue, is the result of a constant suboptimal mediation among different sensibilities. Compromises are the result of patient and persistent rounding of the national interests that influence the perceptions and hamper the resolution of concerns. The former US Secretary of State Henry Kissinger famously spoke of "constructive ambiguity", in the form of manipulations, long procedures, compromises, that made it possible to resolve seemingly intractable stalemates. Modern European integration is a monument to constructive ambiguity – and that should be regarded as a compliment.

In sum, not unlike previous eras of European history, this process of cultural and institutional amalgamation is imperfect and painstaking. It often clashes with equally natural tendencies of differentiation and even disintegration, which resurface time and again when the going gets tough. Consider the experience of the euro crisis, epitomized by Germany's insistence on austerity measures and Greece's inability to implement them. Tabloids photoshopped snapshots of German Chancellor Angela Merkel in Nazi fatigues; innuendoes were made that Greece could meet the demands of creditors only by mortgaging its islands. The vocabulary of European integration is usually centred on the need to accept common rules and take on common burdens in order for all to reap the benefits. Yet, it took a cataclysmic pandemic to move any discussion regarding possible mutualization of public debt beyond some of the most damning cultural stereotyping that Europe has been able to produce.

The North–South divide has created something that I would term "meridionalism". In his celebrated definition of "Orientalism", Palestinian-American scholar Edward Said argued that it "is fundamentally a political doctrine willed over the Orient, because the Orient was weaker than the

West, which elided the Orient's difference with its weakness". It is, he continues, the "distillation of essential ideas about the Orient – its sensuality, its tendency to despotism, its aberrant mentality, its habits of inaccuracy, its backwardness – into a separate and unchallenged coherence".[22] If we replace Orient with South, one gets a general idea of how cultural prejudices have played out in the European public discourse.

In the meantime, the repeated crises that Europe has faced over the past years have forged a more sophisticated and nuanced posture on the issue of debt, structural reforms, and in general the rigidity of rules. The symmetric shock provoked by the pandemic made it more obvious that some structural crises do not have a domestic origin. History will judge whether any European government dealt with Covid-19 better than another. But the point is that the relation between rules and culture is dynamic and not static. The implications of these two factors on a country's governance can be appreciated only if they are seen as two sides of the same coin. In some cases, cultural differences help to explain state performance; in others, rational choices explain successes and failures. In this story, there are no existential dilemmas, but many facts and some prejudice and the study of governance is in fact helpful to resolve them.

Not all that is being said about cultures is wrong. There is no questioning that there exist serious structural weaknesses in Southern Europe, which find their root in specific historical and social traits. Yet, the original sin has been to conceive of the cultural factor as static. There are often outliers that disprove this assumption. Particularly productive regions in unlikely places are described as "Islamic Calvinists" (in Anatolia, Turkey) or "Italian Confucianism" (in the Emilia or Veneto regions), testifying to the symbolic and discursive power attributed to culture in the creation of prosperity.[23] Culture is always present but can be moulded to the social reality that surrounds it.

Yet, Europe has suffered and brought to a calcified extreme a process known as "othering". The Other is the enemy, the mirror image, which in the process becomes constitutive of the self. We define our identity most easily as that which or who we are not. In ancient Rome, which was almost permanently at war, the Other was a potent unifying factor – *hic sunt leones*, "there be lions". The Crusades in the Middle Ages unified Europe against the infidels. In early-modern Europe, the likes of Russia and Turkey have taken turns in constituting Europe's Other, the outer borders of civilization.

One merit of the history of postwar Europe is that integration has once and for all buried "othering" practices within Europe. Europe's principle Other, argues Danish political scientist Ole Wæver, is its own past of war, tyranny and poverty.[24] France and Germany, as a result, are no longer mortal enemies rivalling for Europe's dominance. They are the closest of allies, and at most presenting alternative visions of peace and security in Continental Europe. If one manages to cancel the noise of tabloids and backbenchers' ranting, the government of the United Kingdom leaving the European Union on 31 December 2020 will hopefully and ultimately favour a narrative of "our European friends and partners", not of a perfidious continental Other, bent on ripping Great Britain off or apart.

It is precisely seismic events such as Brexit, Covid-19 or the euro crisis that should caution against taking Europe's achievements for granted. Cultural differences are to be factored in as permanent, constantly changing and constitutive of our polities. If we manage to do that, we will have reached a point where European antinomies will no longer be conceivably framed as othering; European rivalries will not be presented as humiliating caricatures. When that happens, then, perhaps, the invisible Crystal Curtain of cultural stigmatization that descended across a united Continent will be finally shattered and common sense prevails in Europe after all.

4

Hail to the mandarins: the scaffolding of governance

The pursuit of governance is hardly a modern preoccupation: the fourteenth-century Sienese painter Ambrogio Lorenzetti titled one of his iconic frescos "The Effects of Good Government". A bustling construction site, the chatty merchants, a hosiery shop, a handful of patrolling soldiers, a teacher and his students, dancers and artists: had Lorenzetti also painted a physician's waiting room and a retirement community, his "allegory" on government would have anticipated the welfare state by some hundreds of years.[1]

When colours, forms and composition remain so vivid and powerful, they provide a better rendering of governance than a hundred scholarly articles. Indeed, to come up with an agreed definition of "governance" is a hopeless cause. In some languages, the word is untranslatable altogether. In some neo-Latin tongues, the term is simply referred to as "government", which places emphasis on the domestic level and executive power. In a rather standard definition, the World Bank defines governance as: "the traditions and institutions by which authority in a country is exercised. This includes the process by which governments are selected, monitored and replaced; the capacity of the government to effectively formulate and implement sound policies; and the respect of citizens and the state for the institutions that govern economic and social interactions among them".[2]

In other interpretations, governance is a more performative exercise, which finds its realization in the practices and perceptions on governing rather than in any specific action or mechanism. Not unlike Lorenzetti's fresco, it accounts for the "effects" of government for citizens, practices that we recognize in everyday life.

Over time, our understanding of governance has coalesced into a more cohesive body of practices. The casual observer of public policy will likely have heard of the "Washington Consensus". The phrase, originally coined by economist John Williamson, is associated with the set of economic and social policies prescribed by lending institutions, as well as most Western governments, upon delivering financial assistance abroad. The choice of the word "consensus" entails the acceptance of a worldview that puts its faith in liberalization of services and goods, fiscal discipline and deregulation.

Just as importantly, the term has long been associated with its presumed global exportability: the gradual convergence of nations divided by different cultures and political traditions around a common normative template and standards. It was never self-evident that this now familiar blend of prescriptions was ever "consensual". On the contrary, the doctrine sparked fierce popular and intellectual resistance from many quarters, which in the decades before and after the millennium turned into a social, "no-global" movement, opposing its neoliberal ethos.

Perhaps as a result of this visceral hostility, the term "consensus" caught on. Over the past decade a "Beijing consensus"[3] has emerged to describe the version of social and economic progress spearheaded by China over the past three decades. Also in this case, the term has a dubious intellectual coherence, but it has come to represent a governance experience that, contrary to what one might expect in a country ruled by the Communist Party, is not guided by ideology, but by a technocratic mandarinate. Despite the growing criticism for its corruption and "princeling nepotism", the ability of the Party to rule over the world's most populous nation is often praised for its efficient, self-correcting nature: "meritocracy at the top, democracy at the bottom, with room for experimentation in between", say admirers.[4]

Surely enough, placed squarely between the Washington and the Beijing consensus, a "Stockholm consensus" has also emerged. British analyst Mark Leonard qualifies it thus: "nothing less than a new social contract in which a strong and flexible state underpins an innovative, open, knowledge economy. This contract means that the state provides the resources for educating its citizens, treating their illnesses, providing childcare so they can work and integration lessons for newcomers. In exchange, citizens take training, are more flexible and newcomers integrate themselves".[5]

As such, this is not a new thesis and as we have seen in the previous chapters, it is not devoid of some glaring failures. Yet, the overarching feeling remains that this "consensus" amounts not to a socioeconomic model, as Leonard posits, but to a mode of governance. The real consensus concerns the right equilibrium between accountability and effectiveness. It revolves around, on the one hand, the continuing need for an effective and meritocratic administration of public goods and, on the other hand, it must heed the ever-more pressing demands for popular participation. As Nicolas Berggruen

85

and Nathan Gardels have persuasively argued, it is a balance between "tightening up" and "lightening up".[6]

Having situated the cultural fault-lines in Europe in the previous chapter, the next step is to focus on its operational capacity, which is to say the ability of governments to formulate and implement policies. This is what I call the scaffolding of governance. I shall tease it out in this chapter by dwelling on the principle and practices of bureaucratic autonomy, particularly within Europe. I highlight the centrality of bureaucratic autonomy and its variations by focusing on the case of labour-market reforms in Italy, as compared to its Danish model and original.

The lights that darken

No matter how it is defined, the governance gap in Europe is damning. Taking into account some of the more comprehensive indexes measuring a total of 14 indicators related to domestic governance, the results speak for themselves (see Table 4.1).

Like similar other cross-country elaborations, these surveys are unable to capture and nuance the deeper economic and social fabric of a governance structure, including how perceptions are formed within each country and how the assessments of experts differ across time and space. However, they enable us to roughly visualize the differences in performance between Northern and Southern member states of the European Union. According to the World Bank's governance indicators, for example, the best Southern performer, Spain, scores 15 percentage points less than Germany, the closest

Table 4.1 Governance indicators

	Governance indicators*	Sustainable governance**	Quality of government***	Corruption perceptionsΔ
Finland	98.33	77.9	98.14	90
Sweden	97.54	82.9	96.29	88
Denmark	94.78	79.0	97.0	90
The Netherlands	95.79	68.4	94.44	84
Germany	89.30	68.4	88.88	79
Spain	74.71	60.3	75.0	65
Portugal	76.62	57.6	73.14	63
Italy	66.26	56.2	56.94	42
Greece	58.50	45.4	61.11	36

Source: Author's own elaboration of data from the World Bank, the Bertelsmann Foundation, the University of Gothenburg, Transparency International. Where necessary, results have been rescaled as percentiles, with 100 indicating a perfect score.[7]

Notes: *Results here are an aggregate for the six World Bank's governance indicators, measuring voice and accountability; political stability and absence of violence; government effectiveness; regulatory quality; rule of law; control of corruption. **The Bertelsmann Foundation's sustainable governance management index measures a government's steering capability, policy implementation, institutional learning and accountability (http://www.sgi-network.org/index.php?page=scores&category=MD). ***The University of Gothenburg's quality of government index measures corruption, law and order and bureaucratic quality (http://www.qogdata.pol.gu.se/codebook/codebook_standard_15may13.pdf). Δ Transparency International's corruption perception index, "ranks countries and territories based on how corrupt their public sector is perceived to be" (http://www.transparency.org/research/cpi/overview).

Northern performer. The gap between the Netherlands and Greece is over 35 per cent. With regards to corruption perceptions, Nordic countries regularly make the top ten list in Transparency International's index; Italy ranks 69, between Montenegro and Bosnia.

At the heart of this gap is the other legacy of Max Weber, less contested than the one on Protestant ethics, that qualifies bureaucracy as the most mature form in which political authority has historically manifested itself. After the traditional authority of patriarchs and religious leaders, and the charismatic model where authority is presented as a divine gift, bureaucratic authority is the true determinant of a modern state. Bureaucracy is meritocratic, tenured and hierarchical.[8] Underpinning these qualities is a crucial, structural factor that the governance literature refers to as "bureaucratic autonomy". Bureaucratic autonomy, says political scientist David Carpenter, occurs "when bureaucrats take actions ... to which politicians and organized interests defer even though they would prefer that other actions (or no action at all) be taken".[9] States are better governed when the bureaucratic autonomy of its civil service is protected by a political coalition. Bureaucracy is perceived as being impartial, effective and is entrusted with implementing policies in the name of the common interest.

Bureaucratic autonomy is thus the scaffolding of governance. In the more virtuous cases, an autonomous bureaucracy has historically played a systemic role in state-building processes. Bo Lidegaard explained it thus: "'Good governance' in Danish means that you need complete transparency and consistence in the way you serve the citizens. That is because the welfare state is built on rights of the individual ... Under the law, the bureaucracy is obliged to be sure that you get exactly what you are entitled to, no more and no less".[10] In Northern Europe, it seems, Weber is alive and well.

Governance failures, on the other hand, are tied to the absence of bureaucratic autonomy: clientelism, more or less pervasive forms of political patronage which, even when they do not qualify as outright corruption, mix private and public interests and hamper efforts at creating a merit-based administration of the state. Phenomena such as nepotism and cronyism entangle conflicting private interests to the sound administration of the state. The result is a clientelistic system that is the real reason behind the stagnation and lack of reform in, for example, Southern Europe.

An anecdote can help to clarify this crucial difference. A few years ago in Denmark, the literary sensation was a journalistic investigation by Jesper Tynell entitled *Mørkelygten*, which would translate as "the light that darkens". Tynell focused on "scandals" that have to do exclusively with bureaucratic autonomy: he takes a few case studies, from unemployment benefits to the decision of the Danish government to join the US-led invasion of Iraq, to single out situations in which the state bureaucracy interpreted laws or data in a selective way to serve the political master of the day.

He calls this "the art of counting backwards": the politician declares something publicly, and civil servants have to scramble for the evidence and sometimes manufacture connections to support it. In doing so, they deferred to politicians, rather than the common good. The title of the book is aimed at showing situations in which bureaucracy had to "enlighten" things that were useful for politicians, while deliberately obscuring the totality of the picture from public view.

Now let us hop on a two-hour flight South. At around the same time that Tynell was pointing his finger at the Danish bureaucracy, the undisputed best-selling book in Italy was an investigation by two journalists, Gianantonio Stella and Sergio Rizzo entitled *La Casta*, which translates as "The

Caste".[11] Stella and Rizzo's is a story of privileges of the ruling class and of corruption. Also in this case, the book focuses on a number of critical cases. It focuses on the waste and plunder of resources, abuses of power and a systemic culture of impunity in the Italian public sector.

Mørkelygten and *La Casta* focus on the very same topic: the efficiency and flaws of the public service. But they do it in two vastly different national contexts. It is no exaggeration to claim that the Danish public would read "The Caste" as an entertaining story of fiction. Similarly, it is quite likely that the Italian reader would have a very hard time to understand where the "scandal" is in the "Light that Darkens": a case of a bureaucracy that is not slow or corrupted, but that it is so efficient that it overreaches in what it is supposed to do.

This comparison may be extreme, but it does underscore the extent and the ways in which bureaucracy's actions are seen as legitimate and should be held accountable. A bureaucracy that is somewhat insulated from political pressure and popular passions is, almost by definition, not supposed to subject itself to the kind of scrutiny that citizens can exercise towards democratically-elected bodies. Civil servants serve the common good: in a democracy, when there are options or political alternatives, it is ultimately elected politicians that need to decide. But especially in high-profile decisions, the bureaucrat may be conflicted between serving the political masters, the bureaucracy itself or the law. The answer in Europe's North ought to be that the civil servant always serves the law above anything else.

Paradoxically, in this respect, the pursuit of better governance standards is not even correlated to the strengthening of democratic institutions. We do not use the word mandarin accidentally: many of our standards of bureaucratic performance are measured against the Chinese tradition of meritocratic access to public service. China was the first country in the world to have organized a public competition for bureaucrats in the third century BC. The meritocratic access to public service in China is a hallmark of bureaucratic performance, but hardly that of democratic governance.

Discussing cases of authoritarian governments such as Singapore or China today, Francis Fukuyama notes that governance is in fact concerned with "a government's ability to make and enforce rules, and to deliver services, regardless of whether that government is democratic or not".[12] In *The Third Wave*, Samuel P. Huntington further elaborates:

Elections, open, free and fair, are the essence of democracy, the inescapable sine qua non. Governments produced by elections may be inefficient, corrupt, shortsighted, irresponsible, dominated by special interests, and incapable of adopting policies demanded by the public good. These qualities make such governments undesirable but they do not make them undemocratic. Democracy is one public virtue, not the only one, and the relation of democracy to other public virtues and vices can only be understood if democracy is clearly distinguished from the other characteristics of political systems.[13]

Transposed in the European context, framing governance in terms of bureaucratic autonomy impinges on the long-running dispute on the democratic "deficit" of European decision-making. In this reading, bureaucratic autonomy of

EU technocrats delivers on the "output" legitimacy, typically associated with the concrete benefits and results that the EU delivers to citizen. However, especially in times of crisis, this highlights the problems with a lack of "input" in the form of democratic legitimation.[14] Even in Northern Europe, the public debate frequently rages around the seemingly unaccountable power bestowed upon the bureaucratic apparatus.[15]

This perceived lack of accountability of bureaucrats further fans the flames of mutual recriminations in Europe. Fukuyama goes as far as claiming, controversially, that democratization is in fact responsible for the different governance performances in Europe's North and South. In his reading, better governance standards in Europe's North can be attributed to a relatively late arrival of progressively broader suffrage, which enabled the state to build a solid and cohesive structure. In many ways, this is a story that resonates with other Western European experiences of nineteenth-century state formation. One of the main consequences of the advent of the liberal *Rechtsstaat* was the creation of a modern bureaucracy: this was the case in Britain, with the emergence of a meritocratic civil service after the 1853 Northcote-Trevelyan report; it happened in Napoleonic France;[16] and it had happened a century earlier in Prussia, where King Frederick II was "the first servant" of the state.

On the other hand, Fukuyama's argument is that in places like most of Southern Europe, democracy arrived, in relative terms, too soon in the course of the state-building process. Wars, dictatorships or violent revolutions were replaced overnight by elections and democratic representation, leaving large chunks of the state apparatus up for murky, clientelist exchanges.[17] It is a controversial thesis because it corroborates the impression, sometimes echoed in Southern Europe, that Spain or Italy were better off under Franco or Mussolini. Even so, factual experience endorses this controversial assumption. Lucas Papademos, the technocrat who at the end of 2011 was called in to run Greece, reminisces about his experience in government: "The aim is to improve coordination and ensure continuity of policy implementation. Lack of continuity is part of the problem. Some of the staff, particularly those involved in surveillance of policies, should be permanent and not change every time a new government comes into power".[18]

That view is perfectly justifiable. In fact, the qualities described by Papademos correspond to what used to explain the popularity of the EU itself, especially in Southern Europe: delivering what distrusted state institutions proved unable to deliver. Fittingly, Southern governments are often those that need to suspend democratic accountability in order to pass legislation in critical times. This was the case during the euro crisis.

During the emergency created in March 2020 by the Covid-19 pandemic, the countries in Southern Europe that paid the highest toll in terms of casualties and infections effectively had their governments rule by decree for months on end, and impose a wide range of restrictive measures not seen since the Second World War. In Northern Europe, on the contrary, a precondition for the introduction of these measures was either a clear time limitation or a strong, deliberate emphasis on parliamentary oversight.

These examples help to illustrate some of the broader consequences of the governance divide in Europe. A focus on governance has the merit to overcome the dualism between culture and rules: both are real, present and determine the

93

effects that our governments deliver. Yet, a focus on governance also warns against the futility of any serious attempt at comparing or standardizing cultures and rule-making: it leads straight to a bottleneck, which resides in the quality of state performance. Remember, European integration was supposed to be a leveller; it was meant to smooth the sharp corners of national differences and bring countries closer to each other. Ortega y Gasset's adage: "Spain is the problem, Europe is the solution" applied to all of Europe because it solved problems and stepped in wherever national governments could not cope. A decade of crises, from the euro crisis to the pandemic, required all Europeans to go back to the drawing board.

The Italian job

The fallacies exposed by the gap in governance standards reveal what is probably the most dangerous myth of all: convergence. Convergence is the modern-day equivalent or rather, the latest instalment of, the historical diatribe over cultural alignment and confrontation discussed in the previous chapter. In Europe, we measure governance standards and performances as objectively as possible and make the appropriate disclaimers about the limitations of these measurements. But one should make no mistake about the endgame: the point of measuring is that, in the long run, countries coming from very different starting points are supposed to improve and gradually "converge". Convergence will make it easier for them to trade, exchange, travel. It will make it possible for different countries to offer comparable standards of services or goods. In this respect, convergence has to governance the same flaw that the "End of History" had for liberal democracy: a messianic determinism of what the future is supposed to look like.

It is not accidental that the European Bank for Reconstruction and Development, one of the premier institutions supporting and monitoring transition towards market-based liberal democracy entitled one of its annual reports "Convergence at Risk".[19] For all its successes, European integration has not yielded a convergence of outcomes in key policies and reforms. In fact, the belief that countries will ultimately converge into an ever closer Union has plateaued and passed its zenith.[20] More than inspiring a gradual convergence, fiscal discipline has provided a straightjacket containing an uncontrolled rise of public spending of the kind so often done for short-term political calculation.[21]

Yet, a prevailing view, for example in Northern Europe, is that for convergence to make sense, it has to apply not only to fiscal discipline but also to structural reforms of the economy, in things ranging from liberalizations of products and services to labour-market policies. Overall, however, the kind of fiscal convergence brought about by austerity measures has made it harder for the countries subjected to it to make the necessary investments and reforms to achieve convergence in other fields. Worse still, often austerity policies have hampered the state's ability to deliver some critical public goods, as was dramatically proven in relation to healthcare services and infrastructure during the Covid-19 pandemic.[22] The fact of the matter is that once spending cuts are carried out converging on structural reforms has proven a daunting task.

Just as importantly, convergence requires a common mindset of what we understand as state capacity and as the ultimate objectives of structural reforms. The case of labour-market reforms in Italy and its comparison to Denmark is paradigmatic of this conundrum. After delivering on urgently needed measures of budget consolidation after the euro crisis, the government headed by economist Mario Monti since 2011 was tasked with tackling a long-awaited reform of Italy's labour market. International institutions and investors had long pointed at the "duality" between protected, long-term contracts, granted mostly to more senior staff, and precarious and fragmented short-term contracts, mostly for the young. The duality was seen as a major hindrance to the country's competitiveness and a key factor in Italy's failure to lower stubbornly high unemployment rates, hovering around 12.6 per cent and up to 42.9 per cent for those under 25. Monti himself was an admirer of the Danish model: "its society, economy, and civility". The labour-market reform was inspired by aspects of the "flexicurity" model of Denmark's labour market-policy,[23] designed precisely at increasing labour mobility and flexibility in hiring, while expanding workers' security net and retraining programmes.

The negotiation that led to this reform, which continued into the successor governments, including the one headed by Matteo Renzi, was not smooth, marred as it was by special-interest vetoes over individual aspects of the reform package. After months of acrimonious haggling, business leaders stuck to their position that the government's proposals for easing redundancy rules were not bold enough. Trade unions viewed the reform as being underfunded. The financial markets responded to the ensuing uncertainty with renewed upward pressure on Italian borrowing costs. In order to overcome opposition and pass the legislation, the government had to water down its proposals. This pertained especially to the level of policy formulation, where the government was forced to ease firing restrictions and increase costs for temporary hiring only slightly. This deficiency was combined with serious implementation flaws, particularly in relation to the proposed boost to apprenticeships, modelled on the German experience, with both unions and employers dismissing the proposal because of the excessive bureaucracy involved with apprenticeships.

The outcome of that reform is regarded as a half-baked hybrid by independent observers. The Renzi government put forward a new "Jobs Act" (in English in the original) which, among other measures, included a reduction of the typologies of short-term contracts, a rationalization of the labour code, and a gradualism whereby job security increases with seniority.[24] More controversially, the government reduced the scope of the statute of workers dating back to 1970, particularly in its provisions concerning the employers' obligation to rehire an employee dismissed without a justified cause. The proposal was hailed by the private sector, EU institutions and international investors,[25] and harshly criticized by unions and left-wing segments of the prime minister's own centre-left Democratic Party.

The assumption of this reform process was that it is possible to adapt virtuous practices across different national and institutional contexts. Although policy makers and independent observers have repeatedly lauded the virtuosity of labour market reforms in Northern Europe, the argument that best practices can be transplanted in different countries is not as such, Italian: the European Commission has itself adopted "flexicurity" as its ideal type of labour-market reform, and of "post-crisis Europe's new social model".[26] When seen in this light, Southern European governments are not, in effect, "converging": they are encouraged to reform around a set of practices that take their inspiration from the better performing Northern Europe.

This design flaw is the original sin of convergence. While I am not a labour-market economist or lawyer, the case of the Italian Jobs Act and the inspiration to its Danish original helps me to delineate at least three cross-cutting consequences, that have to do more precisely with the scaffolding of governance and its limitation.

For one, the example of the Italian Jobs Act underscores the acute cultural differences in the way of negotiating and resolving conflicts. In line with the Nordic "culture of conversation" that I illustrated earlier, labour relations in Northern Europe are underpinned by well-established practices of consensus. In Italy, the term corresponding to labour-market negotiations ("*concertazione*") has in fact derogatory connotations, as it perpetuates destructive dynamics between employers, trade unions and government. Not incidentally, Renzi at the time argued that it led to a "quagmire" in policy and to the perpetuation of privileges by well-protected social groups.

However, any reform inspired by flexicurity requires cooperation and consensus. The zero-sum adversarial approach chosen by the Italian government may have been necessary in order to pass legislation. But it immediately raised questions about how framework legislation will be translated into actual policy measures both by the bureaucracy, the unions and employers. Not incidentally, after the reform passed in Italy, the rating agency Standards & Poor's lowered the country's credit rating instead of raising it, with the explanation:

"we see a risk that the secondary legislation, which specifies the implementation of provisions in the Jobs Act, could be weakened. We believe this could happen if the government encounters increased opposition from constituencies adversely affected by its policies".[27]

This leads to a second point, about policy implementation and enforcement. In the public debate surrounding Italy's reforms, there is virtually no trace of discussion on the experiences in "model" countries of Europe's North. The "flexicurity" equilibrium in its Nordic version, for example, is maintained by a sophisticated and well-funded system of active labour market policies, aimed at training the unemployed with a view to their reintroduction in the job market.[28] The careful combination of flexibility, security and active labour market policies are considered by specialists as an integral part of the "golden triangle" of flexicurity.[29] In Europe's South, and in Italy in particular, existing instruments for retraining the workforce are mired in criticisms that are directly correlated to poor governance: active labour market policies are poorly managed and underfunded.

More damning still, Southern European reform overlooked that active labour market policies are criticized in the North as well: they are costly, inefficient, with implementation often outsourced to private consultancies which contribute to an Orwellian scenario of obsessive and obtuse state control. Anecdotal evidence brings back memory of temporarily unemployed research colleagues forced into weeks of full-time training, enlightening them in the art of editing their resumés. In the words of Mette Frederiksen, then Danish minister for employment and the current prime minister: "we take the courage away from adult people by sending them to pointless activation courses. We have to use money on what works, not on controlling or harassing people".[30] Had such comparisons taken place in Italy, it would be easier to substantiate the effectiveness of proposals and anticipate hurdles.

Third, and most importantly, there is the question of outcomes and effects on the labour market itself. The results of the Italian Jobs Act have been mixed and were overcome by the politicization that followed them. As two labour-market specialists have noted: "Labour market flexibilisation brought a sharp increase in fixed-term contracts and a decline in real wages. However, these structural reforms have contributed to reducing Italy's productivity growth. Labour market liberalisation generated temporary jobs. However, cheap labour reduced real wages and diminished incentives for companies to make labour-saving investments – with negative effects on productivity, which is the basis for long-term growth".[31]

What is more, the Act has not changed the fact that Italy continues to have one of the lowest levels of labour productivity in Europe, which has in fact been in continuous decline over the past 20 years. In a study about Italy's declining labour productivity, University of Chicago economists Bruno Pellegrino and Luigi Zingales conclude that "we find no evidence that this slowdown is due to the introduction of the euro or to excessively protective labor regulation ... Familism and cronyism appear to be the ultimate causes of the Italian disease".[32]

This extends also to the institutions meant to implement something like the active labour market policies that are meant to bring "flexicurity" to life. Instructive in this regard is an episode recounted by the Swedish political scientist Bo Rothstein and involving Gösta Rehn, the labour economist and later official at the Organization of Economic Cooperation and Development who "invented" the Swedish model of active labour market policies. He travelled across Europe in the 1960s advocating the system. When in Italy, "his Italian hosts thought that everything looked very interesting in the model world, but when he broached the subject of how it should all be organized, they began to smile".[33]

Crudely compared, the 40 hour (37.5 hours, to be precise) working week in Denmark is almost "net" of transactions, negotiations and haggling. Whereas, the 40 weekly work hours in Italy are "gross", loaded and slowed down by red tape, arcane rules, an opaque private sector or the filibuster of trade unions. You need to minus much of the above before actually beginning work. The point is not that policies are good or bad; it is whether they produce the same results in different countries. In the case of labour-market policies, the answer is no, and the reason is clientelism, the widespread practice of entangling conflicting private interests in the administration of the state, of regarding citizens and public officials as "clients".

This is not something we can easily get around, and it is something that has been grossly unappreciated in the European experience. If the past decade in Europe has taught us anything, it is that when looking at the results we need to factor in inherent differences among countries. Difference is a most misunderstood value of the European experience. French philosopher Jacques Derrida famously saw in Europe's *différance*, the making of a hybrid category of the political, where diversity becomes constitutive of a new socio-cultural whole.[34]

When seen through the lenses of actual governance experiences, the reality is much more mundane. Europeans have succeeded whenever they have accepted that deeper factors, whether organized along national or functional lines, are in fact non-negotiable. Any prospect of cooperation has to accept this reality and indeed work around it. If there is one universal lesson from the modern European story it is not in convergence or in its diversity with a capital D. In a genuine middle way fashion, it is in its ability to accommodate and live with differences.

5

The good disorder: the limits to governance

The room is cramped, the air is stale, the nylon carpet dotted with coffee stains. The setting is the Bella Center, a clumsily named conference facility in the suburbs of Copenhagen. Outside it is a freezing December evening, and the 2009 United Nations summit on climate change is just about to spectacularly collapse. The gathering in that room was not even supposed to take place: with a snowstorm incoming, the Indian prime minister had already announced his departure for the airport. But there he still is, deep in conversation with the Chinese Premier, the Brazilian president and his South African counterpart. US president Barack Obama peeps in and pops an innocent, five-word question: "Are you ready for me?" There was no space at the table, recounts a reporter, so Brazil's president "squeezed round allowing Mr Obama to pull up a chair and sit down".[1]

"Copenhagen" has since become a byword for global discord. Whatever the five leaders talked about back in 2009, it did not save that most hyped and inconclusive of meetings from miserable failure. The summit, colloquially known as COP15, had effectively collapsed months before it even started, under the weight of irreconcilable differences between the North and South of the world.

Climate deniers had long been at work to disparage the urgency of an agreement on carbon emissions. If not in its substance, then certainly the form the summit took was reflective of a cynical stance: I, for one, had never seen so many gas-guzzling, armoured SUVs bulldozing through Copenhagen as in those two fateful weeks. Compounding a general sense of anarchy, surprisingly poor organization left delegates by the thousand freezing outside an overbooked conference centre. Stories of heads of state unrecognized by security guards and sent to the back of the entrance queue made the rounds on the internet. To top it all, the ultimate irony during a negotiation on rising temperatures: it was absurdly cold. In the midst of this mayhem, Obama's polite request to join that conversation with the other heads of government would appear a routine act of courtesy. In reality, it better serves as the unwitting formula of the new world disorder.

The climate deluge might have mattered less if it had not come to mark so neatly the reaching of a tipping point. In the ensuing years not a week has gone by without some kind of postmortem being published on the Western way of life. Obama's successor at the White House further precipitated America and the world into a post-Western world. A plethora of new actors, from Asian mandarins to billionaire philanthropists, has joined the top table of global decision-making and they all seem intent on squeezing Western powers out. The liberal institutions that Europe and America moulded out of the rubble of two world wars appear to have exhausted their purpose. On that December night, it became patent that alternative sources of global power exist, but just like hedge-fund managers or the members of China's Politburo, they are faceless to most of us. What we make of it, for now, is a general sense of inexorable disorder.

Gone are the days when a more arrogant American president would have strode into the room and dictated conditions to anyone in attendance. Gone are the days when Chinese and Indian leaders would barely be on speaking terms and would compete for the title of standard-bearer of the Third World. In fact, long gone are also the days of the Third World, which today is being rapidly replaced by a varied cast of emerging economies. In 2008, as he accepted the Democratic Party nomination for president, Obama had promised that: "This was the moment when the rise of the oceans began to slow and our planet began to heal". But in Copenhagen, that prediction rang embarrassingly hollow: it is not only the natural elements that are beyond our control, but what happens inside a room next door.[2] You can almost picture it: like Obama, we pace up and down the corridor, perhaps chewing some nicotine gum. The West nervously waits for others to tell us what to do. Are they ready for us? But ready for what? Who are "they"? And above all: how did we get to this point?

Paraphrasing the British historian Eric Hobsbawm, the new century has brought us something of a "short two decades", defined by three seminal events. The first was the 2001 terrorist attacks on the United States; the second is the 2008 collapse of Lehman Brothers investment bank; the third the Covid-19 pandemic of 2020. Before these calamitous 20 years, the world had coalesced around a consensus, where the pre-eminence of the United States in the military, economic and cultural realms was unrivalled. The triumph of democracy that followed the collapse of the Soviet Union turned America's primacy into a sort of benign hegemony.

What followed the fall of the Twin Towers was two-trillion dollars' worth of wars in Afghanistan and Iraq. America was arguably made safer from the terrorist threat but the utter debacle of the conflicts and ensuing nation-building projects in both countries alienated allies and fortified adversaries. Lehman's fall exposed years of reckless financial engineering and ushered in the worst financial crash since 1929. The crash rapidly morphed into a credit crunch and then into a global economic slump consisting of renationalized industries, squeezed middle classes and millions of people on the streets – protesting, unemployed, or both. The maelstrom engulfed the rest of the world, and most dramatically Europe. At the time of writing, the global spread of Covid-19 seems to have shattered our borderless way of life altogether.

This chapter lifts our journey in the pursuit of governance to the global level of analysis. It provides an overview of the complexity of governing practices in a multi-polar world. It then views these through the lenses of "neo-medievalism", not quite a theory as much as a metaphorical lens through which scholars and practitioners have observed the deeply intertwined and inherently disorderly fashion of contempo-rary global interaction. It concludes by pointing out that such a narrative has the merit of highlighting the limitations of multilateral schemes as well as offering unlikely cues for their renewal and reform.

The improbable routine

For all the truths that the virus has shattered and all the uncertainty that it has created, the pandemic does seem to provide validation and acceleration for the changes that the world had witnessed before Covid-19 erupted. The United States under Donald Trump was retrenching in a stubborn and erratic response, made up of changing strategies and empty threats. China has for a time emerged victorious from its battle against the virus. Citizens the world over placed their hopes on emulating aspects of the successful authoritarian lockdown by Beijing and on its timely ability to dole out state-led support, sanitary equipment, and medical advisers to countries in need. An unstoppable trend towards de-globalization seems now perfectly attuned to the almost identical sequencing of border closures, travel bans, lockdowns and curfews enacted by country after country.

Compounding this predicament is the emergence of a world the West had not expected to see. In less than 30 years, China's GDP has grown tenfold and its economy is now expected to overtake that of the United States by the year 2028.[3] Singapore's per capita GDP is already 20 per cent higher than that of the United States. So characteristic is India's ability to direct cutting-edge scientific advances to the needs of developing societies that specialists speak of "Indovations".[4] In Brazil income inequality remains as extreme as the skyscrapers built next to the *favela* in Sao Paulo's Morumbi district. Yet, during the past decade, Brazil had become a contributor to overseas development assistance to the tune of US$4 billion a year, a figure comparable to that of charitable Northerners such as Sweden and Canada.[5]

To quantify the world's shift, no measure is more eyecatching than the ability of an economy to actually make things. In 1970, the American share of world manufacturing production was almost 30 per cent against China's less than 4 per cent. By 2012, China overtook America, by accounting for about 20 per cent of the world's total against America's 17 per cent.[6] Optimists may argue that America's inevitable transition to a service economy accounts for this shift. Manufacturing costs in China are rising, innovation in high-end goods is lagging behind and output is still inextricably tied to the West's ability to innovate and consume. But over the past three decades, all basic indicators of China's economy have been rising relentlessly.

For the full picture, consider International Futures, an integrated global modelling index developed by the University of Denver that measures global political and economic influence as a composite sum of national wealth, defence spending, population growth and technological innovation in a given country. According to the model, which is used by the likes of the US National Intelligence Council and the European Commission, the clout of the United States as a percentage of global power decreases from about 22 per cent in 2005 to 18 per cent in 2025; Europe collectively goes down from 17 to 13 per cent. China and India, conversely, rise from 12 to 16 per cent and from 7.5 to 10 per cent respectively.[7]

Decline may be a matter of perception, but these snapshots do hammer home a rather uncomfortable point: today's irresistible rise of the East and of the South of the world appears to come at the expense of the West's established position of primacy. This is no litany about the limits to growth or about a looming zero-sum game between winners and losers in today's world; it is straightforward number crunching of the twenty-first century. Throughout the last century, military might used to be the most revealing indicator of a nation in ascent. In imperial Japan a century ago, for one, you would have heard that rich nations build strong armies. Today, the growth of China's military spending raises eyebrows, but it is less of an immediate concern for the man and woman in the Western street than are the implications of Beijing's rise for jobs and balance of payments in Europe or the United States.

Another adage, however, is still also valid, erroneously attributed to Voltaire but later appropriated by Spiderman: with greater power comes greater responsibility. One would expect that the growing clout of emerging economies would also entail an agenda for how to run the affairs of the world. But for all the alphabet soup bringing together different collections of countries in wishful or imaginary alliances, there is little bringing these powers together. From Brasilia to Beijing, one hears echoes of the non-aligned "developmentalism" dating back to the Cold War era; China's growing financial assistance to and stealthy penetration of the domestic affairs of several African countries may be realizing just that. But we do not see new Gandhis or Mandelas to lead them.

China, one will argue, has set up an ambitious Belt and Road initiative, reimagining the Silk Road of centuries ago around a vast global programme of infrastructural development connecting China to the world. But quite aside from the fact that a pandemic stemming from China itself has altogether revolutionized travel and communication patterns, the Belt and Road has not translated so far in a value proposition that is an alternative to democratic governance. At the outset of the financial crisis, the West responded to calls for a more balanced setup of global governance by expanding the G8 group of major economies into a G20, including emerging powers. But that forum too has lost its shine a decade following its elevation. In keeping with climate change, the so-called

G-77 movement championed by China brings together the world's developing countries. But the world's worst defor- ester, Brazil, is hardly going to have the same priorities of its biggest afforester, China.[8]

The result is an increasingly amorphous diffusion of power in the world. Whatever follows US primacy is not a rational redistribution around a handful of identifiable centres. Nor have the much-maligned "coalitions of the willing" that fol- lowed 9/11 rolled back to traditional multilateralism based on inclusive institutions such as the United Nations. The United States and China are rivals, but their financial systems and trade flows are deeply interwoven. Russia is unlikely to become "westernized" any time soon, but the past decade has only led the West to court Moscow more assiduously. The world is not bipolar, as during the Cold War; nor is it "unipo- lar" as in the glorious 1990s. Attributes such as "non-polar", "G-zero" and "post-American"[9] have been coined to describe the global power shift. This flurry of prefixes is telling of our historical phase of transition: our age is defined more by the preceding ones than by any distinctive quality of its own.

This jungle of overlapping terms does testify to the obso- lescence of the global order that emerged after the Second World War. The UN, the International Monetary Fund, the World Bank represented a world exhausted by war and crav- ing reconciliation with a finished product. To a large degree, these organizations carry the ideological markers of Western modernity, as a well as a membership where Westerners are overrepresented. But today's general assemblies of the world hardly command the respect of the odd rogue state; legalis- tic proceedings are bypassed or ignored, when not paralyzed from the outset. They have been replaced by smaller groups of like-minded countries in ad hoc constellations that serve minimal, often single issue, purposes.[10]

What we are left with is an endemic insecurity about our future. In the best of cases this translates into a fascination with the "improbable".[11] Economists cite the work of mathematician Benoit Mandelbrot to demonstrate the likelihood of financial epidemics and other cataclysmic events. We shiver at our chronic lack of preparation and imagination. We evoke "Black Swans", which are supposed to be extremely rare occurrences with systemic effects; but we evoke them *all the time*. "The 21st century has seen so many examples of 'the unthinkable'," quipped *The Economist*, "that the unthinkable is now routine".[12] Be that as it may, the unthinkable need not equate to something to be pessimistic about. The one lesson from Denmark after COP15 is that there is no inevitable correlation between disorder and disaster. What if, on the contrary, our current dearth of certainties was to turn to our advantage? What if the West were to advance in spite of decline? "We are gliding into disorder", observed Lebanese-American author Nassim Taleb "but not necessarily bad disorder".[13] What if disorder is indeed for the good?

Our medieval future

The musical album as a coherent artistic whole has lost much of its appeal. Listeners increasingly buy individual tracks on various platforms on the internet; and that is when they actually pay for listening. Enter *The Future is Medieval*, released by the British pop band Kaiser Chiefs in 2011. This is the first bespoke record, where customers decide the playing order of the tracks, choose a cover for the album, and can make a profit by reselling their own version online. At one stroke, the Kaiser Chiefs threw 30 years of cultural criticism on its head. Collective narratives, we are told, are systematically parcelled, customized, and then consumed. Postmodern Western individualism has pervaded our psyche; we have created a "culture of narcissism", as a 1979 bestseller proclaimed.[14] But if you cannot beat these trends, Kaiser Chiefs seem to suggest, you have to join them; let us channel our need for attention to do something that others may use and even enjoy.

It could be argued that the Nordics have done something similar to global governance. They are used to global disorder, or to be more precise, they are used to coexisting with the disorder of others. From Dag Hammarskjöld to Greta Thunberg, the Nordic region has over the decades built a reputation for diplomatic balance, humanitarian equanimity, and international peace: a sort of secular conscience of the world. It is, after all, a Norwegian committee that awards the Nobel Peace Prize and the Swedish Academy that awards all the others. During the Cold War, the neutrality of the Nordic countries served the world as an oasis of common sense; from Reykjavik to Helsinki, it was an ideal and very real place where East and West could meet halfway. That is why political scientists have coined the term "security community" to characterize how a sense of community and dependable expectations of peaceful change have made war impossible in this part of the world. But it was not always like this. To understand how they accomplished this feat, we need to reach further back in time.

We do not normally associate the attribute "medieval" with something positive, let alone something happening in

112

the future. It was an age of Western decline but, no differently to today's world order, the West presented only one, biased, side of the story. In Asia, for example, the Middle Ages were anything but a dark age. The Chinese are rightly proud of the ingenuity of the Middle Kingdom in designing mechanisms ranging from the first mechanical clock (in AD 1086) to the first printing press with movable type (some three hundred years before Gutenberg). Ming China sponsored the voyages that took Admiral Zheng He all the way to the Arabian Peninsula and the Eastern coast of Africa – almost a century before Vasco de Gama travelled the same routes in the opposite direction. Marco Polo's ecstatic reports from thirteenth-century China showed Europeans that another, brighter, world existed beyond the narrow confines of their introspection.

As we witness the supposedly unstoppable ascent of today's China, it is only appropriate that a medieval parallel has emerged to reveal the hidden qualities of a declining age. A global era characterized by the West's diminishing reach does in some respects resemble the state of affairs during the age of Dante's life. His was a world in which the general make-up of Western Christendom was in practice characterized by a plethora of deeply interwoven, and increasingly influential, power players. Medieval Europe was an environment populated by emperors and popes, city states and corporate actors. It was a system that is hard to decipher to this day, in which alliances were made and broken, but still one that remained interconnected, somewhat structured, and extremely fluid. Then as now, corporations and religious institutions decisively influenced the affairs of sovereigns. Then as now, private security contractors, sovereign wealth funds and universities filled whatever vacuum could be found in the political space.[15]

The Covid-19 pandemic has made the parallel even more poignant, with the Black Death in the fourteenth century killing as much as 40 per cent of the English population and decimating the city of Florence, which lost half of its inhabitants. For all the uncertainty that Covid-19 has created, the medieval comparison also offers a stark contrast. As historian Yuval Noah Harari argues:

People had no idea what causes it and what could be done about it. Until the modern era, humans usually blamed diseases on angry gods, malicious demons or bad air, and did not even suspect the existence of bacteria and viruses. People believed in angels and fairies, but they could not imagine that a single drop of water might contain an entire armada of deadly predators. Therefore when the Black Death or smallpox came to visit, the best thing the authorities could think of doing was organizing mass prayers to various gods and saints. It didn't help. Indeed, when people gathered together for mass prayers, it often caused mass infections.[16]

Another silver lining is in the way Northern Europe adapted and averted the uncertainties of medieval disorder. In the twelfth century, the Hanseatic League created a thick network of city states, ranging from the Eastern coast of the Baltic Sea, in today's Russia, to the west in today's Netherlands. In an age in which the nation-states were either not formed or were just about to emerge, the Hansa constituted a formidable network centred on the export of goods such as timber and corn, transported from Central and Eastern Europe by river, and then moved to the rest of Europe via the Baltic Sea. To this day, one only needs to compare the main squares of cities such as Lübeck in Germany, Gdansk in Poland, Riga in Latvia, to recognize the unmistakable markers denoting Hanseatic allegiance.

In time, the Hansa gained almost a monopoly of trade in Northern Europe. The key intuition was that going through the sea route rather than the land route was faster and safer. The League gradually declined when some kingdoms, particularly Denmark in the sixteenth century, took over the prerogatives typical of nation-states, for example through the imposition of tolls and tariffs on the Hanseatic cargos. In an epilogue eerily familiar with the world of today, a brutal series of protectionist measures hampered, and eventually ditched, the Hansa's successful free-market operation. Yet, the myth of the Hansa lived on. After the Cold War, all the countries of the Baltic area pulled together making an explicit reference to the innovations of the Hansa. Today the Northern European countries of the EU, brought together by similar sentiments in relation to liberalizations and foreign trade, have formally constituted themselves as the New Hansa.[17]

Today's "medievalism" does not amount to a coherent reading of the world. But it provides a lens through which to look at the important megatrends of our age. The most defining of these has certainly been globalization. The seamless flow of capital, goods, people and ideas worldwide has been the most striking feature of the past 30 years. In the early post-Cold War era, globalization seemed to equate to Americanization in all walks of social, economic and cultural life. But as US global reach recedes and Brexit Britain takes on a quest to "take back control", a number of tenets under-pinning globalization have started to shake. Take economic integration: as America is gripped in a seemingly unresolv-able trade deadlock with China, governments threaten or raise trade barriers to prevent corporate takeovers by foreign companies on grounds of national security.[18] Populists of all stripes advocate a return to mercantilism and protectionism as a way of defending Western economies from the downsides of free trade and open markets. Globalization has turned from representing the zenith of Western liberalism into something of a Frankenstein's monster.

Medievalist fans will tell you that this story of partial "de-globalization" has a more constructive side. For one, global challenges do not always require global solutions. Consider, again, pollution. Dreadful experiences such as the Copenhagen climate summit remind us that we have learnt to view the environment as an eminently global phenom-enon: government strategies and research programmes, Greenpeace and the WWF, all tend to refer to the whole planet as the object of our concerns. Globalization is precisely what makes us part of this common discourse. The world ought to be responsible for "Our Common Future",[19] as a milestone UN report once put it, because there is "no Planet B".

However, global problems always produce effects that are much more delimited in space. Viruses for example do not respect borders and the pandemic was consequently global; but the measures adopted to tackle it differed in every coun-try and world region. The environment may be global, but the challenges that people face, let alone natural disasters, are much more restricted in focus. To present the case of ris-ing sea levels, you might have seen sophisticated computer animations about very local phenomena, such as the submergence of the Maldives or the flooding of Manhattan. Similarly, a shipwreck occurring in the Mediterranean is not going to prompt the Japanese coastguard to come to the rescue. Social scientists call this "re-territorialization".[20] Certain issues may be global, but their response is local. Responsibility and competences find their optimal territorial dimension and so, to some extent, does our sense of belonging. As sixteenth-century Dutch jurist Hugo Grotius wrote: "For as a ship may attain to such a size that it cannot be steered, so also the number of inhabitants and the distance between places may be so great as to not tolerate a single government".[21]

The composite nature of participation in the global arena has allowed for other medieval parallels. One is urbanization: in Asia alone, 44 million people join city populations each year. Every day sees the construction of 20,000 new dwellings and 250km of new roads. The world's top 100 cities account, by some measures, for 30 per cent of the world economy: London, New York and Paris alone are worth more than 40 economies of sub-Saharan Africa combined.[22] Yet, from Lagos in Nigeria to India's megalopolises, cities are also the tragic sites of entire communities lacking adequate housing, sanitation and jobs. In another medieval parallel, urbanization is a mirror of income inequality. This notwithstanding, the rise of local authorities heralds a move towards governance carried out at the level closest to the individual. The Roman Catholic Church, that most medieval of institutions, first came up with the idea. As Pope Pius XI explained in the 1930s: "Just as it is gravely wrong to take from individuals what they can accomplish by their own initiative and industry and give it to the community, so also it is an injustice ... to assign to a greater and higher association what lesser and subordinate organizations can do".[23]

Today, this principle – called "subsidiarity" – is applied in multilevel structures such as the European Union. It does not always result in an effective division of labour: in medieval as in modern times, the rise of different levels has led to autonomies, exceptions, mixed allegiances and overlapping loyalties. But this patchwork of authorities resonates with today's world, where it is not only nations that hold rights and responsibilities, but everything and everyone who claims a place in the global arena. This intricate dynamic of power is detectable when a security contractor controls immigration flows,[24] when governments intervene in the market through the creation of "rainy day" funds or indeed, when philanthropists have the smartest and most effective solutions to tackle climate change.

The underlying question, however, remains: is this kind of world a nice place to live in, or not? No matter how we look at it, this medieval parallel does not change, in fact it reinforces, the perception of relative decline of the West. From systemic economic failures and the rise of Asia to mass migration and man-made or natural disasters, we look at the future with angst. Of course, we can hail the coming of a new Renaissance.[25] But compounding a perception of decline with one of disorder does not create the ideal conditions for a thriving civilization; it conjures up uncertainty and fear.

The political thinker Hedley Bull seemed to think otherwise. In his 1977 masterpiece, aptly titled *The Anarchical Society*, he was among the first to theorize the emergence of a new medieval world. When it comes to the desirability of such a world, he says, it all boils down to what we mean by "order". "Order", Bull explains, "is necessarily a *relative* concept: an arrangement (say, of books) that is orderly in relation to one purpose (finding a book by a particular author) may be disorderly in relation to another purpose (finding a book on a particular subject)".[26]

For the best part of the last century, Karl Marx's *Das Kapital* would have offered principles of absolute order for about half of the world's surface. In medieval Europe, the Church would have read the solution to most disputes straight out of the Bible. Today, absolute sources of order are disappearing as fast as actual libraries. But in the Middle Ages as in today's world, this does not change the fact that we yearn for some kind of ordering. "Order in social life", Bull acknowledges, "is desirable because it is the condition for the realization of other values",[27] things such as peace, prosperity, toleration and justice.[28] We may choose to catalogue books in a library differently, we may choose to digitalize them and dismantle the library altogether; but what matters in the act of cataloguing is that it facilitates us to find what we are looking for.

For today's world, and for each of us within it, it is no different. Whether we are in a global pandemic or a climate disaster, what we cherish is not order as such; we cherish what order enables us to attain. It is of no comfort to know that order is a matter of perception; whatever your perspective, what matters is what it delivers. Western decline, be it real or just perceived, has delivered a sense of disorientation. A medieval-like environment may be confusing at first; but it also provides a silver-lining to harness the values that we cherish the most. Relinquishing global primacy may lead to uncertainty and self-doubt; but it can also force us to focus on hard facts and zoom in on what really matters. Let me turn to how that might concretely happen.

6

A transnational world: the practice of governance

Let us go back for a moment where this journey started, in Copenhagen. After that disgraced climate summit of 2009, most governments would have probably lain low for a while. At a time of economic downturn and austerity, it was not apparent that climate investments were an "insurance policy" on the future, as the Danish government kept billing them. Even for an obsessively eco-friendly public, it was not self-evident why Denmark or Europe should take a worldwide lead on climate, when no-one else is there to follow.

Yet, the tiny kingdom hosting that tragic display at the Bella Conference Center begged to differ. Denmark had made of climate policies a hallmark of its global image; what issue could be better to brand a small nation at the top of Europe than saving the planet from deliberate self-destruction. After such a debacle, anyone would be forced to reconsider priorities. But over the past decade Denmark's climate policies have been nothing if not ambitious. Since the COP15 summit failure, Copenhagen first reached its greenhouse gas emissions reduction targets at 20 per cent in 2020, then raised them to 40 per cent for 2030. Officials have no qualms in admitting that meeting this objective required heavy public investment. But after it outpaced its own 2020 target of reaching a 30 per cent share of renewable energy, Denmark set a 55 per cent target for 2030. A broad cross-party coalition has ensured the goal of phasing out all fossil fuels production by the year 2050. In 2019, Copenhagen set out to become the first carbon neutral capital in the world by the year 2025.

Where it gets interesting is in the means necessary to support these policies. There are the familiar things, such as improving efficiency and extending financial incentives in renewables. But Denmark is also seeking ways to stimulate innovation and to make green investments attractive for companies. Together with South Korea and Mexico, in 2013 Denmark launched a Global Green Growth Forum (3GF) to marry bottom-up ideas from corporate and research actors with top-down government support. Companies such as Samsung, Siemens and General Electric joined forces with the likes of University of California, Berkeley and WWF, aided by governments that pledge to create a stable environment for green investments. Civil society, businesses and the media are part of the endeavour at all times.

Since 2018, the 3GF has become the P4G (Partnering for Green Growth and Global Goals 2030) bringing together 58 countries, over 140 business partners, and 100 civil society actors, all working on 50 concrete projects aimed at "pioneering market-based partnerships to build sustainable and resilient economies",[1] on anything from Africa's renewable energy markets to leveraging economic systems aimed at cutting food loss and waste by a half.

Denmark could not but resign to the failure of the climate summit, but rather than giving up or holding back, it decided to double down. It concentrated on narrow objectives where the interests of diverse actors could gather. Not unlike

Marquis Childs' middle way, it has opted for an informed, meticulous search for consensus, "made of practical steps fulfilling multiple purposes", as one of the architects of the Danish climate policy privately told me. Buried somewhere in the subconscious, such strategy may be rooted in a dream to save the planet. But the goal of creating "market-based partnerships" allows little time for starry-eyed idealism. It is about "making money", no different than how FDR put it in relation to the original Swedish experiment with cooperatives, but with a moral purpose that is just as noble.

This pragmatism, simplicity, and even modesty walks on the beaten path of the Nordic middle way. But it need not be an exclusively Nordic quality. The reader who has been patient to read thus far will have noticed that one of the leitmotivs of this book is that to take a virtuous governance model (Nordic or any other, for that matter) and attempt to transplant it elsewhere is methodologically faulty and intellectually futile. There are very many reasons why, say, Southern Europe is not like Northern Europe: clientelism, corruption, inequality, tax evasion, mistrust. Citizens and policy makers in those countries are perfectly aware of them. Touting a role model will only add insult to injury. As a foreigner living and working in these fortunate lands, I have always noticed how Nordics are acutely weary of bragging about any "model".

That is why this book has set out to do the opposite exercise: it has worked deductively, taking concrete practices, such as labour market reforms in Denmark or a summer festival in Sweden, or the response to Covid-19 in the Nordics and sought to put the results in a general context about their significance for the future of governance. This is also what I set out to do with the story of Denmark's climate debacle and its remarkable comeback.

As rock poet Patti Smith once wrote: "Often contradiction is the clearest way to truth".[2] The proof that global governance can work in practice anywhere in the world has to be proven as far away from the ideal as one can possibly go. I shall therefore consider a case, which is as representative as it is extreme of effective transnational governance, going quite literally to the world's "Heart of Darkness". I shall then tease out of it a handful of principles that can guide the formulation of sound policies relevant for the governance of the future.

Blood diamonds

As with much else in Rome, Adriano's jewellery store is all about presentation. After closing a sale, he wraps the engagement ring in a deep-blue package and seals it in burgundy-red wax. He handwrites the warranty with a fountain pen on parchment paper and muses over the diamond's four "Cs": colour, clarity, carats and cut. As with much else in Italy, something odd is always around the corner; in this case, capping this baroque ceremony with the austere formula: "the diamond you purchased was procured through legitimate sources, not involved in the financing of conflicts, and in full compliance with United Nations resolutions". The customer gone, Adriano turns to me and confides, "For eight out of ten of them, it really matters to know that they didn't buy a blood diamond".[3]

Trade in conflict diamonds has been a scourge of Western policy makers for decades.[4] And yet the way diplomacy managed to solve it is often used – together, in fact with the case of climate governance – as the textbook case of effective transnational governance.[5] This illegal commerce is long acknowledged to have fed the finances of warring parties and irregular guerrilla combatants in diamond producing regions, especially in Africa. As American journalist Greg Campbell argued with reference to the conflict in Sierra Leone of the late 1990s: "The [war] was conducted not for any ideological dogma, noble cause or even for retribution by a long-aggrieved people, but purely for the economics of diamond mining".[6]

In a business such as jewellery, estimated to amount to up to $300 billion in annual revenues worldwide (over a third of which generated in the United States), it is not hard to appreciate how diamonds can turn into an arsenal. In the 1990s some 90 per cent of diamond revenues in Sierra Leone bypassed the government and exited the country through illicit channels. In a comprehensive study of the subject, Matthew Hart estimates that although Liberia's official annual diamond production in the mid-1990s amounted to some 150,000 carats, its real exports to Belgium (the city of Antwerp being a critical hub for the diamond industry) amounted to some 12.3 million carats. Between 1992 and 1997 alone, the Angolan rebel militia amassed some $3.7 billion in diamond revenues. Differently to gold, drugs or almost anything else you can think of smuggling, these figures have been made possible only because diamonds are small and odourless, "the most portable form of wealth known to man".[7]

Over the past two decades, the practices by which militias have extorted and traded diamonds have made headlines. Film makers have portrayed in lurid detail stories of rebels amputating the arms and legs of civilians, of young women reduced to sexual slavery, of drugged child soldiers responding to *noms de guerre* such as General Babykiller or Queen Chop Hands.[8]

Even terrorists of various persuasions have invested in diamonds in order to protect the wealth that they have accumulated. In a November 2001 investigation, the *Washington Post* uncovered a direct link between the Sierra Leonean rebels and Al Qaeda's cell in Kenya. Hezbollah, the powerful Shia militia, which the United States lists as a terrorist organization, has been able to count on a community of over 100,000 Lebanese based in West Africa, many of them businessmen involved in the commerce of diamonds.

In all these accounts, the elephant in the room is typically the diamond industry. Through ubiquitous publicity and careful control of the market, diamond suppliers have been instrumental in creating and maintaining the myth associated with the gem. Cecil Rhodes, the founder of diamond giant De Beers, had it all figured out at the very beginning of the company's fortunes, in the 1880s. His empire, he noted, was safe as long as "men and women continued to fall in love".[9]

Today, the diamond market is made up of a handful of large companies carefully controlling supply. As gross human rights violations occurred as a result of the diamond trade, it is inevitable that the de facto cartel practices of the industry are singled out for criticism. The Rhodesian smuggler portrayed by Leonardo DiCaprio in the Hollywood blockbuster *Blood Diamonds* offers a pitiless charge against the diamond industry: "You control the supply and keep the demand high. [If] the rebels want to flood the market with a billion worth of rough, a company saying that [the stones] are rare can't afford to let that happen. Especially when they are telling some poor sod that he is supposed to shell out three months' salary for an engagement ring. [Technically] speaking, they are not financing the war, but creating a situation where it pays to keep it going".[10]

In the late 1990s pressure began to mount. Global Witness, a British NGO, launched a number of campaigns on conflict diamonds, which would earn them a nomination for the Nobel Peace Prize.[11] In the United States a coalition of humanitarian groups put together a "Campaign to Eliminate Conflict Diamonds" and urged consumers to be aware of the provenance of their gems. A consumer boycott became a distinct possibility. "Added to the famous four Cs of diamonds ...", Global Witness cleverly put it, "should be a fifth – conflict".

The rot was primarily rooted in the fact that the origin of stones could not be credibly certified. "It was apparent to a number of countries", explains Clive Wright, a British diplomat involved in the process, "that a thin patchwork of national certification schemes would be insufficient to tackle conflicts".[12] Meeting later that year in Kimberley, South Africa (the location of Cecil Rhodes' first mine), 35 representatives of governments and NGOs involved in the production, distribution and export of diamonds initiated the "Kimberley Process". As mandated by the United Nations, this group would be tasked to agree upon an international certification scheme for rough diamonds. Shortly after, the US Congress adopted a Clean Diamond Trade Act. In the wake of the 9/11 attack – and just three weeks after the *Washington Post* report had linked conflict diamonds to Al Qaeda – the US House of Representatives passed the bill with a vote of 408 to 6.[13]

In November 2002, Kimberly Process members introduced the certification scheme. The idea is simple: if a country does not adhere to strict control standards, member countries refuse to trade diamonds with it. Broad participation in the scheme is therefore a crucial success factor. To date, some 82 governments have joined the Process, including most of the

major diamond producing countries, as well the main consumers: the United States, China, Russia, Brazil, India, and the
European Union with all its member states. NGOs like Global
Witness and the industry including, crucially, De Beers, have
been essential participants in the mechanism throughout and
have joined the Kimberley Process as observers. It is never
easy to measure success in political affairs, but some facts
cannot be disputed. At the time of the Process's inception,
diamond trade attributable to conflict amounted to 4 per cent
of the world total; one year after Kimberley's implementation,
that proportion fell to less than 1 per cent. Two years on, it was
down to 0.2 per cent.[14]

Still, some see the glass as half empty. Kimberley is a volun-
tary exercise, where few sanctions can be applied, and compliance and verification are left to peer pressure. Moreover,
modern technology notwithstanding, identifying the precise
origin of a diamond is a tricky business. Practitioners will
tell you that an expert eye can distinguish the provenance
of a stone, but certifying the origin beyond doubt is virtually impossible. "While the Kimberley certificate is today's
near-universal standard requirement to trade rough diamonds", writes Norwegian reporter Jason Miklian, "it is still
shamefully basic. It's a single sheet of paper identifying only
the country of origin, the country of import, value and total
carats of each diamond shipment – along with a serial number and a couple of signatures. It's about as easy to fake as an
old driver's licence".[15] Above all, the fall in the trade of conflict
diamonds is not only the result of the international community's do-gooding; it happened principally because the wars
in West Africa have ended. The wars have ended because of
changing dynamics among the warring parties as well as

foreign military interventions, not because of a trade certification scheme.

If anything, the Kimberly Process is as much about showing the limits of governance schemes, as it embodies the management of disorder in a complex environment. But both these severe limits and the peculiar constellation that has emerged around the diamond diplomacy help to single out what makes this case interesting. The horrors of war, trafficking and organized crime compelled policy makers to act. It would have not been inconceivable, or unjustified, if torture, rape and systematic murder had brought down an entire corporation. Kimberley could have been billed as an intervention to stop crimes against humanity. But it was not bleeding-heart altruism that got the ball rolling, just a trade-control measure. And still the little stone sold by some jeweller is the result of a struggle fought in Africa, Asia and the rarefied boardrooms of global diplomacy.

Organic intelligence

Social scientists and international organizations are always ready to coin new terms and brand new concepts. Policy makers speak of the need for coherence, cohesion and coordination. We have global "compacts", getting NGOs, businesses and governments working side by side. "Coalitions" or even "concerts" of various sorts bring different actors together, and when they agree, we have a "consensus". To say nothing about "clusters", so beloved of management gurus. It does not make much sense to coin yet another iteration of these terms. What we know is that any such initiative as the Kimberley certificate can be informed by some big idea, worldview or even ideology, but in the end it will be measured by results and the way in which it responds to concrete and vital needs.

In this respect, rather than inventing yet another label, it may be more useful to reflect on what this case reveals. Thomas Hobbes famously wrote of the state of nature in a pejorative way, the anarchical zero-sum environment of *Homo homini lupus*, the man as a wolf to the other man. While it is true as Hobbes argued that we need a "pact" to settle our basic need for survival, with the benefit of insight, the state of nature itself does at face value not seem more threatening than the post-American world. On the contrary, social scientists have long been attracted by principles of societal self-organization and competition that appear so close to the natural world.[16]

Nature is resourceful and self-reliant. It splits or clumps together depending on needs, transforms itself based on principles of adaptation and survival. Humanity has always tried to imitate nature – from art to engineering. The golden ratio used by architects and mathematicians codifies what we see in nature, whether it is a shell or the human body. No other term embodies our quest for reproducing the way nature works as much as "resilience", our need to: "live with change and uncertainty; nurturing diversity for reorganization and renewal; combining different types of knowledge for learning; and creating opportunity for self-organization toward social-ecological sustainability".[17]

For organizations and institutions, it is no different. One remarkably effective, if morally deplorable, example of self-organizing and resilient social system is organized crime. In the words of the Italian parliamentary commission on the

Mafia organization stemming from the southern region of Calabria: "it has a tentacular structure, devoid of any strategic direction but characterized by some kind of organic intelligence".[18] In a paradoxical way, a world ravaged by natural disasters, pandemics and threatened by a climate armageddon needs some kind of "organic intelligence" to rekindle its priorities and modus operandi. The case of the diplomacy of blood diamonds is not perfect. But if it is often used as a reference, it is because of the way in which it came about and for what it says about the principles that should underpin governance in a disorderly world.

The first principle is that for governance to work in the twenty-first century you have to broaden the typology of actors involved beyond the state but limit their number to the bare minimum. The implementation of transnational policies would be unthinkable without the involvement of a broad selection of players; but complex cooperative endeavours also need to retain a sense of purpose. Multilateralism was the formula of choice to get the Kimberley process to fly; but the United Nations, inclusive and unwieldy, was behind the curve. The real work was carried out by an ad hoc group of governments, industry, media and civil society actors. Without the NGO Global Witness uncovering the scandal, one would probably not have heard about the trade in the first place; without the conglomerate De Beers, any scheme would have been pointless. But the scheme could never have taken off without governments stepping in eventually. In 2000, the three largest diamond-producing countries (South Africa, Botswana and Namibia) liaised with the three main consumers (the United States, the United Kingdom and Belgium) and set the machinery in motion. Washington, in particular, made the necessary leap to give the certification the weight it required. The participation of most other world powers, as well as the EU and other producing countries, gave it scope.

This tripartite model of government, business and civil society is known as the triangle of transnational governance.[19] From the Gates Foundation to the World Economic Forum, to indeed the Danish P4G initiative on climate, many organizations increasingly operate this way as a substitute for unwieldy global institutions.[20] When these partnerships are not formalized, they operate side-by-side to existing formats. The World Bank has a long track record of cooperation with private actors. Independent, non-governmental bodies such as Human Rights Watch or the International Crisis Group provide regular reporting to governments. For better or worse, management consultants have been engaged in trying to optimize the way governments operate even in sensitive areas such as asylum policies.[21]

All the more, the authority and legitimacy of the state remains central: the Kimberley Process would never have got off the ground if exporting and consuming governments had not got their act together. In other instances, the absence of the United States sucks the oxygen out of any global governance endeavour, such as the International Criminal Court. The emergence and success of populist movements throughout the world is, in this respect, a direct backlash to the unwieldiness of international cooperation: if it does not deliver, we have to go it alone. On the other hand, the first principle of transnational governance is that for a dinner party to succeed, one had better select the guests carefully.

The second principle is that the Kimberley process displays what some commentators call, borrowing from the Danish physicist Per Bak, the "sand pile effect". As author Joshua Cooper Ramo summarizes, "if you piled sand, grain by grain, until it made a cone the size of your fist, how would you know when that tiny pyramid would have a little avalanche?"[22] In a system whose individual units are connected to each other, even tiny events, like a single extra grain poured onto the sand pile, will at some point carry consequences for the whole system. The Kimberley Process started out as a very specific measure aimed at controlling the sources of diamonds, but in reality it achieves much more. The likes of De Beers did not enter Kimberley by chance or pro bono; they did it because blood diamonds were hurting business. A trade restriction helps coerce the non-compliant diamond producers to align and may caution the industry on its more haphazard practices. This form of corporate responsibility makes an industry that does not want blood on its stones more credible for investors and customers.

A fair trade of diamonds may also catalyze governance reform in developing countries. The case of Botswana, which depends on diamonds for 85 per cent of its exports, is often singled out by international lenders for its transparent partnership with De Beers and for the independent institutions managing diamond revenues.[23] Botswana's control of diamond mining further shows how good governance helps to beat the so-called "resource curse", which afflicts states blessed by an abundance of precious resources but coupled with corruption and authoritarianism. However, there is really much more. Any one of us who, at one point or another, has bought or received jewellery as a gift is affected. We are all grains in the sand pile, and can very concretely do something, for example by refusing to buy uncertified diamonds. So, the second principle that makes transnational governance worth pursuing is that a tiny event, like buying an engagement ring in a jewellery shop in the suburbs of Rome, is correlated to a cascade of effects in a complex system, sometimes reaching out to the other end of the world.

Third principle: we need someone to help us connect the dots and can afford to say it like it is. Without Global Witness' shaming of industry and governments, it is hard to say when or how the blood diamond curse would have been addressed. Without the *Washington Post* linking this obscure trade to Islamist terrorism, the number one security threat of the day, politicians could have easily ignored the alarm calls. Without DiCaprio putting a face to this ominous plague, millions of people would have forgotten the whole thing by now. We have seen this pattern time and again; after the Rwandan genocide, Hurricane Katrina, the financial crisis and the Covid-19 pandemic: every given tragedy prompts the international community to close ranks under the battle cry of "never again". But it is activists, the media, and even the entertainment industry, which hold the power of turning a seemingly dormant issue into a vital one. They are the "couriers" [24] delivering the message, as well as the agents of urgency.

To be fair, it is not always so clear-cut. Supposedly independent civil society is often accused of lobbying for special interests rather than embodying the general interest. Investigative reporting, indispensable in bringing these stories to light and truly the elixir of a free society, is time-consuming, expensive and increasingly challenged in today's media landscape.[25] Some devastating critiques have followed the invasive presence of celebrities in public policy discussions.[26] But whether you love them or hate them, the role of these couriers is to take matters to the court of public opinion. Democratic governments are accountable to their citizens. Publicly traded companies respond to their shareholders. Civil society has the role of holding power-holders accountable. In fact, if there is one single reason why these disparate segments of society are grouped under the heading "civil", it is probably because they act as the conscience of our values.

Which leads to a fourth and final insight offered by the diplomacy of blood diamonds. The low-profile negotiations took place roughly at the same time as the US-led war in Iraq and could have drummed up some political momentum. The involvement of rogue autocrats, the Al Qaeda connection, and appalling crimes against civilians suggested as much. But the parties chose to stick with the unexciting issue of a certification scheme. Low profile does not mean value-neutral. Since early modern times, trade principles and strategies have influenced or determined the fate of empires. Trade is associated with centuries of pillaging of natural and human resources in Africa, America and Asia; the subjugation of entire populations embodies the white man's shameful "civilizing mission". From David Ricardo to the European Union, trade has represented one of the most distinctive and contested features of Western ascendancy.[27]

Yet, sticking to something as unglamorous as a certification scheme is a choice dictated by calculations of self-interest. Simplifying, this tactic could be compared to the prosecutor's strategies in the trials against Al Capone and against Serbia's strongman Slobodan Milosevic. In the case against Chicago's ruthless mafia boss of the 1920s, the court could not find witnesses brave enough to testify against him, and Capone was famously convicted for tax evasion. In 2002 the former Serbian president was accused on 66 counts of crimes against humanity; prosecutors called 293 witnesses to testify and amassed thousands of pages of documentary evidence. Capone's conviction for fiscal fraud may have not set an obvious example about the fight against organized crime, but it did deliver some justice. In Milosevic's trial, the prosecutor wanted to do justice to all of his victims, yet the trial was so long and complex that the defendant died before a verdict could be reached.[28]

Likewise, a technical issue such as trade restriction is not directly attached to the "greater good". Policy makers did not associate the Kimberley Process to any ethical or normative principle. As the Namibian minister of mines put it: "The Kimberley Process is not a human rights organization". But it is probably fair to say it that in the end it did do more good than, say, a high-minded and ill-fated multilateral enterprise such as the United Nations Human Rights Council. All along, Kimberley's sole goal has been to stem the traffic of illicit stones. Yet, no one could doubt that what was also at stake was the fate of child soldiers. Values are our roots to the extent that they may be invisible, buried underground, but constitutive of any virtuous collective action. Restating them obsessively may only demonstrate how uncertain we really feel about them. What matters is that they provide a solid anchoring to our actions.

The example of diamond diplomacy thus provides four key principles for the future conditions of governance. The case illustrates that grouping private, public and civic actors can work, if they manage to fit and sit around a table – meaning that the numbers are small and the attitude constructive. Then, a self-fulfilling "sand-pile effect" unfolds, where small, seemingly insignificant acts of cooperation reverberate into the most noble values of humanity. The case demonstrates the importance of connectivity and identifies the "couriers" that help to connect the dots: media platforms, civil society, even celebrities. Finally, it underscores the need for pragmatism, to aim for the low-hanging fruits, practical steps fulfilling multiple purposes. It requires a vision of the kind of world we want to inhabit, but it relies on focus, patience and persistence to get there, one step at a time.

Conclusion: a new middle way

"Crawl back under your rock!" There is not much diplomacy left to spare in Margot Wallström. The then Swedish foreign minister will be remembered as one of her country's most respected statespersons of the beginning of this century. She has embodied the values of openness, equality and tolerance that we associate with Europe's North. Among other initiatives, she pioneered a "feminist" foreign policy, to promote equal opportunities in all aspects of Sweden's international projection. And it is precisely in relation to this that she clearly lost her cool. The target of the fury that led her effectively to compare him to a snake is Jordan Peterson, Professor of Psychology at the University of Toronto, who had earned a reputation and a large following for his politically incorrect positions, in particular on gender issues.

Peterson was in Sweden to promote one of his books and found himself entangled in a dispute on equal opportunities with Swedish feminists. Peterson's thesis, which he argues is supported by a quarter of a century of quantitative research in social psychology, is that countries like the Nordic ones which have reached the highest standards in terms of gender opportunities, have produced the most unequal results in terms of actual *choices*, for example in the workplace. In other words, given the best possible opportunity to choose, women tend to select certain kinds of jobs as compared to men, with women usually picking jobs on the lower side of the employment pyramid and men choosing those on the top.[1]

Peterson should have never gone there. The Swedish public, usually civilized and measured, burst into a collective bout
of disdain. But the Canadian psychologist, now stained as a
chauvinist of the worst kind, doubles down: his interpretation
of the data is that the moment the barriers between men and
women are lowered, the biological factor is decisive to explain
gender behaviour and ultimately differences. Put another way,
once the structural constraints disappear, natural differences
between genders emerge, for example in professional settings.
Plainly, this point reinforces stereotyping and discrimina-
tions, such as those that see men more inclined to relate to
objects and mechanics, while women's innate sociability is
reflected in jobs in the healthcare sector.

But there is more to this episode than meets the eye.
Gender parity is one of the most extraordinary achievements
of Nordic societies. Anyone travelling to the Nordic countries
will have noticed this simply by walking to a park, populated
by fathers on long paternity leave pushing strollers and drink-
ing cappuccinos. It is an unwritten code, a mindset, as much
as something enshrined in rules or quotas. One could go as
far as claiming that no foreigner can go about living among
the Nordics without embracing gender parity in all of its fac-
ets. Yet, precisely because it embodies in such fundamental
way the Nordic way of life, the episode involving Wallström
allows me to illuminate one of the most paradoxical conclusions of these dispatches from the future of governance: the
sophistication, and the almost inhuman perfection of Nordic
countries relies on a tightly-knit institutional, societal and
educational fabric to thrive. These factors are tantamount
to an ecosystem that enables a species to survive. When an
intervening factor alters or threatens the ecosystem, Nordics

take no prisoners and the response has to be firm, radical, even brutal.

When seen in this light, perhaps it is no accident that the Nordic literary sensations of the past few years belong to the blockbuster genre of crime novels known as Nordic noir, made most famous outside the region by books like Stieg Larsson's *The Girl with the Dragon Tattoo*. The tensions within Nordic noir novels emerge from the contrast between the apparently bland, conformist social surfaces of the Nordic societies in which they are set and the horrific accounts of murder, misogyny or racism they depict as lurking beneath those surfaces. Some have wondered why a region characterized by such supposed social harmony would produce such dark fictional tales. But this is exactly the point: one reason why Nordic noir fiction is so popular is because of how it reveals contradictions, how the seemingly idyllic and even boring context masks a hidden reality of heinous crimes and moral depravity. In societies that rightly boast of their high standards of gender equality, it is not a coincidence that Larsson's novel was originally entitled, in Swedish, "Män Som Hatar Kvinnor" – "Men Who Hate Women".

This very contrast has recurred throughout this book and constitutes the backbone of the new governance middle way that I have sought to portray. For indeed, as we saw in the first two chapters, a culture of conversation is a precondition to socially construct the "pincer movement" of elites and citizens embracing democratic governance. Yet, the Nordic case suggests that what enables this conversation to take place is the existence of an entry code, made of innate civility and consensus to be sure, but also of socialization mechanisms that are unwritten as they are deeply ingrained, for example in the education system. Without knowing the cyphers of that code, or by deliberately scrambling them, implies automatic exclusion. This might explain the inherent difficulties of migrant communities in integrating in a tightly-knit social fabric; likewise, it may explain the success of right-wing populist movements that rather than presenting themselves as "anti-systemic", hark back and capitalize on those most visceral, tribal sentiments of belonging.

In the third and fourth chapters, I discussed how the Nordic model and particularly its economic and political reforms are admired and emulated the world over, and for sure are a paragon within the European Union. The limit of this emulation has resided in the surprising inability to properly account for cultural differences in the formation of policies and preferences, also within a continent accustomed to diversity such as Europe. This has been particularly evident in the longstanding divide between Europe's North and South and has spilled over into what I have called the scaffolding of governance: namely, the role of the civil service in providing transparency and continuity to policy making and the need for politics to protect its autonomy. Notwithstanding the long intellectual pedigree of ethnographic literature in Europe, the inability to recognize the importance of cultural elements and to account for differences among countries has impaired the successful rollout of key policies. The case study comparing labour market reforms in Italy and Denmark underscored the limitations of applying similar policies in different national contexts.

In the last two chapters, I have posited that transnational governance among governments, civil society, media platforms and business is what makes the Nordic model tick.

It takes place at every level and in every corner, even as the world witnesses a power shift towards Asia and worrying relapses into nationalism. This "neo-medieval" world, where allegiances shift and loyalties overlap, requires a nimble, minimalistic institutional design that not everyone seems to appreciate. The ability to create multicultural, borderless exchanges is the mantra that globalization has created and that the Nordics have wholeheartedly embraced. But when one digs deeper or where controversy arises, what is revealed beneath the humanitarian and do-gooding surface are ferocious survival instincts.

As seen in the remarkable comeback of Denmark since the 2009 climate summit debacle, the Nordics have pioneered transnational governance and turned it into a modern-day rendition of the middle way. Yet as someone who has lived and worked in these lands, I have been adamant to explain that, with the due disclaimers and caveats, this needs not be an exclusively Nordic condition. I have demonstrated this by means of yet another extreme case, that of Africa's conflict diamonds. So deliberately distant from the blissful surroundings of Scandinavia, the resolution of this scourge by the international community shows the contours of the kind of transnational world that we all might want to inhabit. It is a world in which governance mechanisms are fit for purpose when they optimize the number, typology and quality of the participants involved. It is a world that favours the emergence of "sand pile effects", of small actions producing systemic consequences. Media actors and platforms are harnessed to manage responsibly the power of information. Rather than lofty idealism, these governance mechanisms will be relying on pragmatic and precise policy solutions counting on their ripple effects.

These cases and their interpretation have helped me to tease out something at once extraordinary and terrifying about the nexus of liberty and security upon which the analysis has been built. The Nordics have demonstrated that for democratic governance to be resilient, ground rules and goodwill are of the essence; but for it to thrive, it requires systematic, even ruthless pragmatism about what needs to be done, while keeping firmly in sight our normative and moral horizon. If there is one lesson to draw from this Nordic story it is that for our pursuit of governance to endure in the twenty-first century, the nexus between liberty and security has to be rekindled. But in order to renew it, it has to be one that reconciles populism and technocracy.

These are, as we have seen, two sides of the same coin. Populism is not necessarily a persuasion on the right or on the left of the political spectrum; it is a disposition and a mindset that pervades all Western societies: against the mainstream, nuanced judgement, compromise and of course against the establishment, all in the name of "the people". Technocracy is not a faceless Leviathan populated by anonymous administrators in some perennially clouded capital of continental Europe; it is a shorthand of the Orwellian illusion of control and the obsession to foretell the future. Populism stems from liberty, but it over-reached; technocracy harks back to security, but it degenerated. Populism and technocracy are pulling the foundational nexus of democratic governance in opposite directions to the point of breaking it.

Some scholars talk about "techno-populism",[2] a new political logic, clearly present in some new parties, seeking to combine and complement technical expertise with populist insurgency. But technocracy and populism will not become

144

one. This book has argued that the technocratic and populist logics, methods and their dominance in our processes of governing, require a systemic effort at balancing them. These opposing dispositions have not set out to merge but they need to co-exist.

What is being evoked is, then, nothing less than a modern-day re-enactment of the *"Compromesso storico"*, the historic compromise associated with one of the most daring experiments of Europe's fraught political past: the farsighted attempt in the 1970s to ally the centrist, catch-all Italian Christian Democrats to the Communist Party.[3] In the new compromise, technocrats get a shot at regaining the legitimacy lost in over a decade of crises. They can endeavour to change the public perception of discredited institutions such as the European Union, and turn it into a veritable force for transforming society after Covid-19. Populists will need to resist their disruptive impulses and turn them into healthy criticism. The bet is that a grand bargain between them is possible and indeed necessary.

Like many times before, the Nordics are the forerunners, the pioneers. Perhaps it is true that their pragmatism stems back to the Vikings' relentless quest for survival and freedom. Whatever the reason – and I have tried to show a few – these countries and its peoples have been more radical than others in combining populism and technocracy, sometime to the point of overreaching. Thus, at the time of writing, a country like Denmark, which under a Social Democratic government rightly earned praises for its rigorous technocratic management of the Covid-19 pandemic, is passing immigration and citizenship legislation on exclusionary premises that most other countries would attribute to the populist right.[4] In the

Nordic countries, a tax ID number is all that the state needs to trace the minutiae of any one person's biography, from all the medicines you ever bought to the books you borrowed. Citizens in other countries would shiver at this level of technocratic control; yet this is the compromise Nordic citizens accept in exchange for a state that delivers results. At the same time, radical tendencies often verging on intolerance and chauvinism are protected and defended as part of hard-fought fundamental rights, such as freedom of expression.

Marquis Childs' middle way was between communism and capitalism; the new middle way reconciles technocracy and populism insofar as it manages to weigh the legitimacy coming from above, that comes from knowledge, expertise and outcomes, with the one from below, the one that only free citizens can provide. The Nordics remind us that functioning institutions are essential to carry out reforms in a spirit of transparency, accountability and evidence. But they also prove that bringing the populists into the mainstream fold is about turning their iconoclastic zeal into constructive scepticism.

The jury is still out on whether anyone will master the formula to balance these titanic forces; but this recipe does indicate a workable path about the future of democratic governance. And if we are also able to see the glass half full of the new middle way, we can all aspire to the message written on the billboard that until recently met passengers arriving at Copenhagen Airport: "Welcome to the world's happiest nation".

Notes

INTRODUCTION

1. Woodward, *The Comparative Approach to American History*, 302.
2. Quoted in Hilson, "Consumer co-operation and economic crisis", 181–2; see also Ohlsson "Sweden: still the middle way?".
3. Examples include the annual World Bank's *Governance Indicators*, the Bertelsmann Foundation's *Sustainable Governance Management Index*, the University of Gothenburg's *Quality of Government Index*.
4. Childs, *Sweden: The Middle Way*, 168.
5. On the competitiveness ranking, see *The Global Competitiveness Report 2019*; on transparency, see Transparency International's *Corruption Perception Index*; on happiness, see Martela *et al.*, "The Nordic exceptionalism", *World Happiness Report*. Nordic countries occupy also the first five spots in the top-10 of the world's best countries in terms of social mobility; https://www.weforum.org/agenda/2020/01/these-are-the-10-countries-with-the-best-social-mobility/.
6. Fukuyama, "The imperative of state-building". The original formulation of the phrase, however, belongs to two World Bank economists and appeared in Pritchett & Woolcock, "Solutions when the solution is the problem".
7. Sontag, "A letter from Sweden", 24.
8. The OECD's global ranking on life satisfaction indicator, Finland, Denmark, Iceland, and Norway occupy the first four positions, and Sweden ranks seventh; see OECD, *Society at a Glance 2019*.

1 FROM SINGAPORE TO SACRAMENTO

1. Lidegaard & Tassinari, "The same creed: a conversation about Scandinavian democracy".
2. Wendt, "Anarchy is what states make of it: the social construction of power politics".
3. Adler, "Seizing the middle ground: constructivism in world politics". See also Katzenstein, "Introduction: alternative perspectives on national security".
4. Rasmussen, *A Time for Peace: the West, Civil Society and the Construction of Peace Following the First World War, the Second World War and the Cold War.*
5. Adler, "Seizing the middle ground", 323.
6. Neumann, "Regions in international relations theory: the case for a region-building approach", 6.
7. Walt, "International relations: one world many theories", 38.
8. Adler, "Seizing the middle ground", 339.
9. Eriksson, "Observers or advocates? On the political role of security analysts".
10. Laclau & Mouffe, *Hegemony and Socialist Strategy: Towards a Radical Democratic Politics*, 105–145.
11. Yin, *Case Study Research: Design and Methods*, 13.
12. Waever, "Security, the speech act: analysing the politics of a word".
13. Zakaria & Yew, "Culture is destiny: a conversation with Lee Kwan Yew", 111 and 114.
14. Nehe, "Asian style democracy".
15. Judt, *Ill Fares the Land*, 220.
16. For a lively exchange on this point, see Gat, "The return of authoritarian great powers" and Deudney & Ikenberry, "The myth of the autocratic revival: why liberal democracy will prevail".
17. Data and quote from Zakaria, *The Future of Freedom: Illiberal Democracy at Home and Abroad*, 193.

18. Tracy, "High stakes for Calif. Prop 30 Election Day decision".
19. *The Economist*, "Bark if you don't like deficits".
20. Childs, *Sweden*, 50.
21. *Ibid.*, xii.
22. *Ibid.*, 161.
23. *Ibid.*, 116.
24. Quoted in Hilson, "Consumer co-operation and economic crisis", 104.
25. Childs, *Sweden*, 188.
26. Quoted in Hilson, "Consumer co-operation and economic crisis", 104.
27. Milne, "Global threat fails to break spirit of Sweden's labour model".
28. Andersen. *The Three Worlds of Welfare Capitalism*.
29. Putnam *et al.*, *Making Democracy Work: Civic Traditions in Modern Italy*, 122.
30. *Ibid.*, 124.
31. *Ibid.*
32. Pettersson, "Ancient and modern Swedish land tenure policy".
33. Childs, *Sweden*, 120–24.
34. On conflictophobia, see Marklund, "Hot love and cold people: sexual liberalism as political escapism in radical Sweden" and Sontag, "A letter from Sweden", 23–38.
35. Gustafsson, *Problemformuleringsprivilegiet*.
36. Huntford, *The New Totalitarians*, 7–10.
37. Creation of Reality Group (CRAG). "Foucault on Sweden: 'The end of the Human'".
38. Hirdman, "The social engineers, the rationalist utopia, and the new home of the 1930s".
39. Obama, "President Obama endorses Joe Biden for president".
40. Batchelor, "Brostrøm: Grænselukning er en ren politisk beslutning".
41. Bredsdorff, "Sundhedsstyrelsen advarede mod historisk hastelov".

42. Nikel, "Why Sweden's coronavirus approach is so different from others".
43. Paterlini, "'Closing borders is ridiculous': the epidemiologist behind Sweden's controversial coronavirus strategy".
44. Baker, "Sweden's GDP slumped 8.6% in Q2, more sharply than its neighbors despite its no-lockdown policy".
45. Henley, "Sweden spared European surge as coronavirus infections stay low".
46. Milne, "Architect of Sweden's no-lockdown strategy insists it will pay off".
47. Valery, "Disillusionment".

2   IT TAKES AN ISLAND

1. Hermanson, *Monopol och storfinans: de 15 familjerna.*
2. Giridharadas, *Winners Take All: The Elite Charade of Changing the World.*
3. On equality, see for example OECD, "Income Inequality"; https://data.oecd.org/inequality/income-inequality.htm.
4. Markowitz, *The Meritocracy Trap: How America's Foundational Myth Feeds Inequality, Dismantles the Middle Class, and Devours the Elite.*
5. *The Economist*, "In Sweden, billionaires are surprisingly popular".
6. Hilson, *The Nordic Model: Scandinavia Since 1945*, 78.
7. Linz & Stepan, *Problems of Democratic Transition and Consolidation: Southern Europe, South America, and Post-Communist Europe*; Wilson, *Virtual Politics: Faking Democracy in the Post-Soviet World.* See also Freedom House, *Freedom in the World 2019: Democracy in Retreat.*
8. *The Economist*, "*Bolsa Família*, Brazil's admired anti-poverty programme, is flailing".
9. Przeworski & Limongi, "Modernization: theories and facts".
10. *The Economist*, "Narendra Modi threatens to turn India into a one-party state".

11. An overview of the achievement and challenges of Indian democracy can be found in Jayal, *Democracy in India*. The figures in the text are cited by Rachman, "Indian democracy has an ugly side".

12. Speaking at the National People's Congress in March 2012 for the last time as China's prime minister Wen said "I believe China's democratic system will, in accordance with China's national conditions, develop in a step-by-step way, there is no way to stop this"; see "Chinese Premier Wen Jiabao: democracy in China is 'inevitable'", *The Telegraph*.

13. See Rachman, *Zero-Sum World: Politics, Power and Prosperity After the Crash* and Vogel, *Deng Xiaoping and the Transformation of China*.

14. Kopstein, "The transatlantic divide over democracy promotion".

15. Zakaria, "The rise of illiberal democracy".

16. Wolf, "Lunch with the FT: Francis Fukuyama".

17. Thomas Jefferson to John Adams, 1813; cited in Berggruen & Gardels, *Intelligence Governance for the 21st Century*, 49.

18. Caplan, *The Myth of the Rational Voter: Why Democracies Choose Bad Policies*.

19. Jones, *10% Less Democracy: Why You Should Trust Elites A Little More and the Masses A Little Less*.

20. Tassinari & Miller, "Nordic cuddly capitalism: cover story".

21. Simovska & McNamara (eds), *Schools for Health and Sustainability: Theory, Research and Practice*. Springer, 101.

22. Acemoglu, Robinson & Verdier, "Can't we all be more like Scandinavians? Asymmetric growth and institutions in an interdependent world".

23. See for example SITRA's governance statements: https://www.sitra.fi/en/topics/governance/.

24. Murray, "French notaries and the American mortgage crisis", 275.

25. Packer, "The broken contract".

26. Ohlsson, "Sweden: still the middle way?".
27. Eberstadt, "The great society at 50: the triumph and the tragedy". The 1964 Commission's own key recommendations ended up including minimum wage and job training programmes.
28. Zakaria, *The Future of Freedom: Illiberal Democracy at Home and Abroad.*
29. Baker & Glasner, *The Man who Run Washington: The Life and Times of James A. Baker III*, 223–4.
30. Crook, "Obamacare: the result of all politics, all the time".
31. *Borgen*, season 1, episode 10.
32. Koch, "Ordet eller Sværdet".
33. Lindung, "En intervju med Michel Foucault".
34. Sontag, "A letter from Sweden", 26.
35. "Dennis Kucinich on the Iraq Crisis & what the U.S. can learn from Sweden's political diversity", Democracy Now.
36. See Buckley, "Romania: a Balkan imbroglio". I thank former Romanian minister Cristian Ghinea for providing me with insight and data on the Romanian case.
37. World Economic Forum, "Which countries tax their citizens the most?"
38. See also Svanborg–Sjövall, "Privatising the Swedish welfare state".
39. *The Economist*, "Who is shrugging now?".
40. Rasmussen, *Fra Socialstat til minimalstat.*
41. Schultheis, "What right-wing populists look like in Norway: can they avoid the nativism of their European peers?"
42. Queen Margaret II, "H.M. Dronning Margrethe II's nytårstale".

3   THE CRYSTAL CURTAIN

1. Paul Auster and Wayne Wang (directors) *Blue in the Face* (1995).
2. BBC News, "Norway's NRK broadcasts 12-hour wood burning programme".

3. Berggren & Trägårdh, *Är svensken människa? Gemenskap och oberoende i det moderna Sverige.*
4. Cooper, *The Breaking of Nations*, 190.
5. Rifkin, *The European Dream: How Europe's Vision of the Future is Quietly Eclipsing the American Dream.*
6. On solidarity vs liability, see Hewitt, "Eurozone crisis: North versus South". On labour market, see European Commission, "Press release: Employment: vacancy trends reveal growing North-South divide in EU labour market". On competitiveness, see World Economic Forum, "Rebuilding Europe's Competitiveness".
7. Matthijs, "Mediterranean blues: the crisis in Southern Europe".
8. Olson, *How Bright are the Northern Lights? Some Questions about Sweden*, 7.
9. See also *The Economist*, "Economists are turning to culture to explain wealth and poverty".
10. Acemoglu & Robinson, *Why Nations Fail.*
11. Jones, *The European Miracle: Environment, Economies and Geopolitics in the History of Europe and Asia.*
12. Lewis, *What Went Wrong? The Clash Between Islam and Modernity in the Middle East.*
13. Mokyr, "The enduring riddle of the European miracle: the Enlightenment and the Industrial Revolution".
14. Habermas & Derrida, "February 15, or what binds Europeans together: a plea for a common foreign policy, beginning in the core of Europe".
15. Svendsen & Svendsen, "From vikings to welfare: early state building and social trust in Scandinavia".
16. Østergaard, "Lutheranism, nationalism and the universal welfare state: national churches and national identity after the Reformation and the development of the welfare state in the Nordic national states".
17. Tassinari & Vissing, *Living in Denial: The Cultural Factor in European Policies and Politics.*

18. LeGoff, *L'Uomo medievale*.
19. Ferguson, "A world without power".
20. I have discussed and written extensively about these issues with former Danish ambassador Lars Vissing, who is one of Europe's top authorities on Renaissance diplomacy. The following sections are therefore drawn from Tassinari & Vissing, *Living in Denial*.
21. Guicciardini, *Ricordi Civili e Politici*, 28, emphasis added.
22. Said, *Orientalism*, 205.
23. On Islamic Calvinists, see Knaus, "Islamic Calvinists". On "Italian Confucianism", see Fukuyama, *Trust: Human Nature and the Reconstitution of Social Order*, 97ff.
24. Waever, "European security identities".

4 HAIL TO THE MANDARINS

1. On this fresco, the seminal essay is by Quentin Skinner: "Ambrogio Lorenzetti: the artist as political philosopher".
2. World Bank, *Worldwide Governance Indicators*.
3. Ramo, "The Beijing consensus".
4. Bell & Li, "In defence of how China picks its leaders".
5. Leonard, *Why Europe will Run the 21st Century*, 84.
6. The Economist, "What's gone wrong with democracy?"
7. Countries belonging to either group vary in the literature and public debate, depending on the policy alignment or cultural-political outlook. Accordingly, Austria is often included in the Northern European group and Ireland in the Southern one. For the purpose of this sample, I have chosen a straightforward geographical characterization of the North and the South.
8. Weber, *Economy and Society: An Outline of Interpretive Sociology*, 956ff. The qualities sketched above about a modern bureaucracy were specified much further: according to Weber, bureaucracy for example had to have "channels of appeal", "written documents

(files)", an office "separated from the household". And of course, there have to be "specific examinations as a prerequisite for employment".

9. Carpenter, *The Forging of Bureaucratic Autonomy: Reputations, Networks, and Policy Innovation in Executive Agencies, 1862–1928*, 4.

10. Lidegaard & Tassinari, "The same creed".

11. Rizzo & Stella, *La casta. Perché i politici italiani continuano a essere intoccabili.*

12. Fukuyama, "What is governance?"

13. Huntington, *The Third Wave: Democratization in the Late 20th Century*, 193.

14. Moravcsik, "In defense of the "democratic deficit": reassessing legitimacy in the European Union".

15. See Koch & Knudsen, *Ansvaret der forsvandt: om magten, ministrene og embedsværket.*

16. A comparative analysis of nineteenth-century bureaucratic formation in Europe can be found in Kickert, "Distinctiveness in the study of public management in Europe: a historical institutional analysis of France, Germany and Italy".

17. Fukuyama, "The two Europes".

18. Atkins & Hope, "FT interview transcript: Lucas Papademos".

19. European Bank for Reconstruction and Development, *Transition Report.*

20. See also Moravcsik, "Europe after the crisis: how to sustain a common currency".

21. Monti, "Europe's leaders need to back shift on rules on public investment".

22. Kentikelenis *et al.*, "Greece's health crisis: from austerity to denialism"; Hedgecoe, "In Spain, austerity legacy cripples coronavirus fight".

23. Tassinari, "Mario Monti's Nordic dream".

24. Totaro, "Italy's Renzi wins vote on controversial labor law change".

25. Toschi, "Italy's Jobs Act passes the first hurdle".

26. European Commission, "Towards common principles of flexicurity: more and better jobs through flexibility and security"; see also Begg, "Is 'flexicurity' post-crisis Europe's new social model?".

27. See Ratings Direct, "Ratings on Italy lowered to BBB-/A-; outlook stable", 5 December 2014; http://download.repubblica. it/pdf/2014/economia/Italy2014.pdf.

28. Maselli, "Flexicurity in Italy: how far is Rome from Copenhagen?"

29. Madsen, "The Danish model of 'flexicurity': experiences and lessons".

30. Gaardmand, "Rekordmange ledige ender i 'meningsløs' aktivering" [Record numbers end up in "meaningless activation"].

31. Heimberger & Krowall, "Seven 'surprising' facts about the Italian economy".

32. Pellegrino & Zingales, "Diagnosing the Italian disease".

33. Rothstein, *Social Traps and the Problem of Trust*, 11–12.

34. Derrida: *The Other Heading: Reflections on Today's Europe.*

5   THE GOOD DISORDER

1. An account of this scene appeared in different media following the Copenhagen climate summit; see Harvey *et al.*, "A discordant accord".

2. In fact, that the US delegation did not know about the proceedings in those closed-door meetings has since been disputed. A 2014 investigation by *The Guardian* based on the revelations by whistleblower Edward Snowden ascertained that the US National Security Agency was spying on delegates, including other heads of government, before and during the Copenhagen summit; Vidal & Goldenberger, "Snowden

revelations of NSA spying on Copenhagen climate talks spark anger".

3. BBC News, "Chinese economy to overtake US by '2028' due to Covid".

4. Radjou, *India: The Emerging Innovation Giant.*

5. The figures are from: *The Economist,* "Speak softly and carry a big cheque".

6. One of the most comprehensive reference works of data on economic growth is Madison's *The World Economy.*

7. See the International Futures (Ifs) model developed by the Frederick S. Pardee Center for International Futures, Josef Korbel School of International Studies, University of Denver; www. pardee.du.edu. The accumulated data quoted here are presented in National Intelligence Council, *Global Governance 2025,* 11.

8. An exhaustive overview of China's Africa policy is in Brautigam, *The Dragon's Gift: The Real Story of China in Africa.* On the disagreement among the emerging countries see *The Economist,* "The trillion dollars club".

9. Zakaria, *The Post-American World.*

10. Naim, "Minilateralism: the magic number to get real international action".

11. Ramo, *The Age of the Unthinkable.*

12. *The Economist,* "Future shock".

13. Taleb, *The Black Swan: The Impact of the Highly Improbable,* 225.

14. Lasch, *The Culture of Narcissism: American Life in an Age of Diminishing Expectations.*

15. On these three themes see Truman, *Sovereign Wealth Funds: Threat or Salvation?*; Williams & Abrahamsen, *Security Beyond the State: Private Security in International Politics* and Khanna, *How to Run the World Charting a Course to the Next Renaissance.*

16. Harari, "In the battle against Coronavirus, humanity lacks leadership".

17. Khan, "EU's new Hanseatic League picks its next battle".

18. In recent years, one of the most high-profile cases illustrating this tendency was that of the bid by China's National Offshore Oil Corporation to take over the American oil company Unocal. CNOOC eventually withdrew because of political opposition in the United States; see Barboza, "China backs away from Unocal bid".

19. Brundtland Commission, *Our Common Future: The World Commission on Environment and Development.*

20. Forsberg, "Beyond sovereignty, within territoriality: mapping the space of late modern geo-politics".

21. Grotius, *The Freedom of the Seas.*

22. For the figures on Western cities, see Khanna, "Beyond city limits"; for those on Asian cities see *The Economist*, "Asia's alarming cities".

23. *Quadragesimo anno.* Encyclical of Pope Pius XI, 1931.

24. See Gammeltoft-Hansen & Sorensen (eds), *The Migration Industry and the Commercialization of International Migration.*

25. Khanna, *How to Run the World.*

26. Bull, *The Anarchical Society: A Study of Order in World Politics*, 4.

27. *Ibid.*, 96–7.

28. Watson, *The Evolution of International Society*, 14.

6   A TRANSNATIONAL WORLD

1. Partnering for Green Growth and Global Goals 2030; https://p4gpartnerships.org/about-us.

2. Smith, *Just Kids*, 200.

3. Adriano is the author's father and this is a private conversation.

4. The data here are from Grant & Taylor, "Global governance and conflict diamonds".

5. Abbot, "The transnational regime complex for climate change"; Westerwinter, The Politics of Transnational Institutions.

6. Campbell, *Blood Diamonds: Tracing the Deadly Path of the World's Most Precious Stones*, 156.

7. Hart, *Diamond: A Journey to the Heart of an Obsession.*
8. Campbell, *Blood Diamonds,* xv.
9. *Ibid.,* 113.
10. Edward Zwick (director), Charles Leavitt (writer), *Blood Diamonds* (2006).
11. Global Witness, *A Rough Trade: The Role of Companies and Governments in the Angolan Conflict.*
12. Wright, "Tackling conflict diamonds".
13. Campbell, *Blood Diamonds,* 199.
14. Wright, "Tackling conflict diamonds", 702; Walt, "Diamonds aren't forever".
15. Miklian, "Rough cut"; see also Jeffay: "Unprecedented prosecution for Kimberley process fraud".
16. On Social Darwinism, see Axelrod, *The Evolution of Cooperation.*
17. Folke, Colding & Berkes, "Building resilience for adaptive capacity in social-ecological systems".
18. Emphasis added; original article: Ansa News Agency, "Legalità: Ndrangheta".
19. Abbot, "The transnational regime complex for climate change".
20. Samans, Schwab & Malloch-Brown, "Running the world, after the crash".
21. See Stavinoha & Fotiadis, "Asylum outsourced: McKinsey's secret role in Europe's refugee crisis".
22. Ramo, *Age of the Unthinkable,* 48.
23. Wright, "Tackling conflict diamonds", 698.
24. I draw inspiration for this concept from that of the "connectors" described by Malcolm Gladwell in *The Tipping Point: How Little Things Can Make a Big Difference.*
25. For an exhaustive scholarly work on the role of investigative journalism in democratic politics, see Ettema & Glasse, *Custodians of Conscience: Investigative Journalism and Public Virtue.*
26. Ponte & Richey call this "compassionate consumerism"; see their excellent: *Brand Aid: Shopping Well to Save the World.*

27. For a masterful historical overview, including of the more undignified aspects of Western trade practices, see Ferguson, *Civilization: The West and the Rest.*

28. "Milosevic's war crimes trial a 4-year marathon", CNNWorld, 11 March 2006; Stephen, "Comment: Milosevic and the Al Capone dimension".

CONCLUSION

1. For an account of this anecdote, see "'Crawl back under your rock', Swedish foreign minister tells Canadian professor Jordan B Peterson", *The Local.*

2. Bickerton & Invernizzi, "'Techno-populism' as a new party family: the case of the Five Star Movement and Podemos".

3. Gardels, "Technocracy meets direct democracy in Italy".

4. Agence France Press, "Denmark plans to limit non-Western residents in disadvantaged areas".

References

Abbot, K. "The transnational regime complex for climate change". *Environment and Planning Government and Policy* 30:4 (2012): 571–90.

Acemoglu, D., J. Robinson & T. Verdier. "Can't we all be more like Scandinavians? Asymmetric growth and institutions in an interdependent world". NBER Working Paper No. 18441 (2012).

Acemoglu, D. & J. Robinson. *Why Nations Fail*. London: Crown, 2012.

Adler, E. "Seizing the middle ground: constructivism in world politics". *European Journal of International Relations* 3:3 (1997): 319–63.

Agence France Press. "Denmark plans to limit non-Western residents in disadvantaged areas". 17 March 2021; https://www.theguardian.com/world/2021/mar/17/denmark-plans-to-limit-non-western-residents-in-disadvantaged-areas.

Andersen, G. *The Three Worlds of Welfare Capitalism*. Princeton, NJ: Princeton University Press, 1990.

Ansa News Agency. "Legalità: Ndrangheta"; https://www.ansa.it/legalita/static/ndrangheta.shtml.

Atkins, R. & K. Hope. "FT interview transcript: Lucas Papademos." *Financial Times*, 11 March 2012. https://www.ft.com/content/9b3f8d50-70df-11e1-8456-00144feab49a.

Auster, P. & W. Wang (directors). *Blue in the Face* (1995); https://youtu.be/7rq4x2GqBmY.

Axelrod, R. *The Evolution of Cooperation*. New York: Basic Books, 1984.

Baker, P. & S. Glasner. *The Man Who Run Washington: The Life and Times of James A. Baker III*. New York: Doubleday, 2020.

Baker, S. "Sweden's GDP slumped 8.6% in Q2, more sharply than its neighbors despite its no-lockdown policy". *Business Insider*, 14 August 2020; https://www.businessinsider.com/coronavirus-sweden-gdp-falls-8pc-in-q2-worse-nordic-neighbors-2020-8?r=US&IR=T.

Barboza, D. "China backs away from Unocal bid". *New York Times*, 3 August 2005; https://www.nytimes.com/2005/08/03/business/worldbusiness/china-backs-away-fromunocal-bid.html.

Batchelor, O. "Brostrøm: Grænselukning er en ren politisk beslutning". Danish Broadcasting Corporation, 14 March 2020; https://www.dr.dk/nyheder/indland/brostroem-graenseluk ning-er-en-ren-politisk-beslutning.

BBC News. "Norway's NRK broadcasts 12-hour wood burning programme". BBC, 16 February 2013. https://www.bbc.co.uk/news/world-europe-21482313.

BBC News. "Chinese economy to overtake US 'by 202' due to Covid". BBC, 26 December 2020; https://www.bbc.co.uk/news/world-asia-china-55454146.

Begg, I. "Is 'flexicurity' post-crisis Europe's new social model?" *Bloomberg*, 15 April 2012; https://www.bloomberg.com/opinion/articles/2012-04-15/is-flexicurity-post-crisis-europe-s-new-social-model-.

Bell, D. & E. Li. "In defence of how China picks its leaders". *Financial Times*, 11 November 2012. https://www.ft.com/content/903d 37ac-2a63-11e2-a137-00144feabdc0.

Berggren H. & L. Trägårdh. *Är svensken människa? Gemenskap och oberoende i det moderna Sverige*. Stockholm: Norstedts, 2009.

Berggruen, N. & N. Gardels. *Intelligence Governance for the 21st Century*. Cambridge: Polity, 2012.

Bertelsmann Foundation. Sustainable Governance Index, 2011. https://www.sgi-network.org/2020/.

Bickerton, C. & C. Invernizzi Accetti. "'Techno-populism' as a new party family: the case of the Five Star movement and Podemos". *Contemporary Italian Politics* 10:2 (2018): 132–50.

Brautigam, D. *The Dragon's Gift: The Real Story of China in Africa.* Oxford: Oxford University Press, 2009.

Bredsdorff, M. "Sundhedsstyrelsen advarede mod historisk hastelov". *Politiken*, 15 March 2020; https://politiken.dk/indland/art7705096/Sundhedsstyrelsen-advarede-mod-historisk-hastelov.

Brundtland Commission. *Our Common Future: The World Commission on Environment and Development.* Oxford: Oxford University Press, 1987.

Buckley, N. "Romania: a Balkan imbroglio". *Financial Times*, 12 August 2012; https://www.ft.com/content/9a8fa27e-e07d-11e1-9335-00144feab49a.

Bull, H. *The Anarchical Society: A Study of Order in World Politics.* New York: Columbia University Press, 1977.

Burke, E. *The Works of the Right Honourable Edmund Burke.* 6 vols. London: Henry G. Bohn, 1854; https://press-pubs.uchicago.edu/founders/documents/v1ch13s7.html

Campbell, G. *Blood Diamonds: Tracing the Deadly Path of the World's Most Precious Stones.* New York: Basic Books, 2004.

Caplan, B. *The Myth of the Rational Voter: Why Democracies Choose Bad Policies.* Princeton, NJ: Princeton University Press, 2008.

Carpenter, D. *The Forging of Bureaucratic Autonomy: Reputations, Networks, and Policy Innovation in Executive Agencies, 1862–1928.* Princeton, NJ: Princeton University Press, 2001.

Childs, M. *Sweden: The Middle Way.* New Haven, CT: Yale University Press, 1936.

Cooper, R. *The Breaking of Nations.* London: Atlantic, 2011.

Democracy Now. "Dennis Kucinich on the Iraq crisis & what the U.S. can learn from Sweden's political diversity". 13 July 2004; https://www.democracynow.org/2014/7/3/dennis_kucinich_on_the_iraq_crisis.

Derrida, J. *The Other Heading: Reflections on Today's Europe*. Bloomington, IN: Indiana University Press, 1992.

Deudney, D. & G. John Ikenberry. "The myth of the autocratic revival: why liberal democracy will prevail". *Foreign Affairs* 88:1 (2009): 77–93.

Eberstadt, N. "The Great Society at 50: the triumph and the tragedy". American Enterprise Institute, May 2014; https://www.aei.org/wp-content/uploads/2014/05/-the-great-society-at-fifty-the-triumph-and-the-tragedy_102730423054.pdf?x91208.

Economist. "Future shock". *The Economist*, 7 May 2010.

Economist. "Speak softly and carry a big cheque". *The Economist*, 17 July 2010.

Economist. "Who is shrugging now?" *The Economist*, 20 October 2012.

Economist. "Bark if you don't like deficits". *The Economist*, 24 January 2014.

Economist. "What's gone wrong with democracy?" *The Economist*, 1 March 2014.

Economist. "In Sweden, billionaires are surprisingly popular". *The Economist*, 28 November 2019.

Economist. "Bolsa Família, Brazil's admired anti-poverty programme, is flailing". *The Economist*, 30 January 2020.

Economist. "Economists are turning to culture to explain wealth and poverty". *The Economist*, 3 September 2020.

Economist. "Narendra Modi threatens to turn India into a one-party state". *The Economist*, 28 November 2020.

Eriksson, J. "Observers or advocates? On the political role of security analysts". *Cooperation and Conflict* 34:3 (1999): 311–30.

Ettema, J. & T. Lewis Glasser. *Custodians of Conscience: Investigative Journalism and Public Virtue*. New York: Cambridge University Press, 1998.

European Bank for Reconstruction and Development. Transition Report 2013; https://www.ebrd.com/documents/comms-and-bis/pdf-transition-report-2013-english.pdf.

European Commission. "Towards common principles of flexicurity: more and better jobs through flexibility and security". Communication 0359, 2007.

European Commission. "Employment: vacancy trends reveal growing North-South divide in EU labour market". Press release, 24 February 2014.

Ferguson, N. "A world without power". *Foreign Policy* 143 (2004): 32–9; https://foreignpolicy.com/2009/10/27/a-world-without-power/.

Ferguson, N. *Civilization: The West and the Rest*. London: Allen Lane, 2011.

Fogh, R. *Fra Socialstat til minimalstat*. Copenhagen: Samleren, 1993.

Folke, C., J. Colding & F. Berkes. "Building resilience for adaptive capacity in social-ecological systems". In F. Berkes, J. Colding & C. Folke (eds), *Navigating Social-Ecological Systems: Building Resilience for Complexity and Change*. Cambridge: Cambridge University Press, 2002.

Forsberg, T. "Beyond sovereignty, within territoriality: mapping the space of late modern geo-politics". *Cooperation and Conflict* 31:4 (1996): 355–86.

Freedom House. *Freedom in the World 2019: Democracy in Retreat*. New York. https://freedomhouse.org/report/freedom-world/2019/democracy-retreat.

Fukuyama, F. *Trust: Human Nature and the Reconstitution of Social Order*. New York: Simon & Schuster, 1996.

Fukuyama, F. "The imperative of state-building". *Journal of Democracy* 15:2 (2004): 17–31.

Fukuyama, F. "The two Europes". *The American Interest*, 8 May 2012; https://www.the-american-interest.com/2012/05/08/the-two-europes/.

Fukuyama, F. "What is governance?" *Governance* 26:3 (2013): 347–68.

Gaardmand, N."Rekordmange ledige ender i 'meningsløs' aktivering". *Information*, 10 July 2012; https://www.information.dk/indland/2012/07/rekordmange-ledige-ender-meningsloes-aktivering.

Gammeltoft-Hansen, T. & N. Nyberg Sorensen (eds). *The Migration Industry and the Commercialization of International Migration*. London: Routledge, 2012.

Gardels, N. "Technocracy meets direct democracy in Italy". Noema, 19 February 2021; https://www.noemamag.com/technocracy-meets-direct-democracy-in-italy.

Gat, A. "The return of authoritarian Great Powers". *Foreign Affairs* 86:4 (2007): 59–69.

Gert Tinggaard, S. & G. Svendsen. "From vikings to welfare: early state building and social trust in Scandinavia". 14th Annual Conference of the International Society for New Institutional Economics, University of Stirling, 2010; http://extranet.isnie.org/uploads/isnie2010/svendsen_svendsen.pdf.

Giridharadas, A. *Winners Take All: The Elite Charade of Changing the World*. New York: Penguin, 2020.

Gladwell, M. *The Tipping Point: How Little Things can make a Big Difference*. New York: Little, Brown, 2000.

Global Witness. *A Rough Trade: The Role of Companies and Governments in the Angolan Conflict*. London, 1998.

Grant, A. & I. Taylor. "Global governance and conflict diamonds: the Kimberley process and the quest for clean gems". *The Roundtable: The Commonwealth Journal of International Affairs* 93 (2004): 385–401.

Grotius, H. *The Freedom of the Seas, or, the right which belongs to the Dutch to take Part in the East Indian Trade: a Dissertation* [1608]. New York: Oxford University Press, 1916.

Guicciardini, F. *Ricordi Civili e Politici*. (a cura di Raffaele Spongano) [1530]. Florence: Sansoni, 1951.

Gustafsson, L. *Problemformuleringsprivilegiet*. Stockholm: Norstedts Förlag, 1989.

Habermas, J. & J. Derrida. "February 15, or what binds Europeans together: a plea for a common foreign policy, beginning in the core of Europe". *Constellations* 10:3 (2003): 291–7.

Harari, Y. "In the battle against coronavirus, humanity lacks leadership". *Time*, 15 March 2020. https://time.com/5803225/ yuval-noah-harari-coronavirus-humanity-leadership/.

Hart, M. *Diamond: A Journey to the Heart of an Obsession.* New York: Penguin, 2002.

Harvey, F. *et al.* "A discordant accord". *Financial Times*, 21 December, 2009; https://www.ft.com/content/8fb70c48-ed9b-11de-ba12-00144feab49a.

Hedgecoe, G. "In Spain, austerity legacy cripples coronavirus fight". Politico Europe, 28 March 2020; https://www.politico.eu/article/ in-spain-austerity-legacy-cripples-coronavirus-fight/.

Heimberger, P. & N. Krowall. "Seven 'surprising' facts about the Italian economy". Social Europe, 25 June 2020; https://www.social europe.eu/seven-surprising-facts-about-the-italian-economy.

Henley, J. "Sweden spared European surge as coronavirus infections stay low". *The Guardian*, 14 September 2020; https://www. theguardian.com/world/2020/sep/15/sweden-records-its-fewest-daily-covid-19-cases-since-march.

Hermanson, C. *Monopol och storfinans: de 15 familjerna*. Rabénoch: Sjögren, 1971.

Hewitt, G. "Eurozone crisis: North versus South". BBC News, 11 July 2012; https://www.bbc.co.uk/news/world-europe-18793708.

Hilson, M. *The Nordic Model: Scandinavia Since 1945*. London: Reaktion, 2008.

Hilson, M. "Consumer co-operation and economic crisis: the 1936 Roosevelt Inquiry on Co-operative Enterprise and the emergence of the Nordic 'Middle Way'". *Contemporary European History* 22:2 (2013): 181–98.

Hirdman, Y. "The social engineers, the rationalist utopia, and the new home of the 1930s". *International Journal of Political Economy* 22:2 (1992): 22–49.

Huntford, R. *The New Totalitarians*. London: Allen Lane, 1971.

Huntington, S. *The Third Wave: Democratization in the Late 20th Century*. Norman, OK: University of Oklahoma Press, 1993.

Jayal, N. *Democracy in India*. Oxford: Oxford University Press, 2008.

Jeffay, J. "'Unprecedented' prosecution for Kimberley Process fraud". IDEX, 20 October 2020; http://www.idexonline.com/FullArticle?Id=46159.

Jones, E. *The European Miracle: Environment, Economies and Geopolitics in the History of Europe and Asia*. New York: Cambridge University Press, 1981.

Jones, G. *10% Less Democracy: Why You Should Trust Elites a Little More and the Masses a Little Less*. Stanford, CA: Stanford University Press, 2020.

Judt, T. *Ill Fares The Land*. London: Penguin, 2010.

Katzenstein, P. "Introduction: alternative perspectives on national security". In P. Katzenstein (ed.), *The Culture of National Security*. New York: Columbia University Press, 1996.

Kentikelenis, A. *et al*. "Greece's health crisis: from austerity to denialism". *The Lancet* 383(9918) (2017): 748–53.

Khan, M. "EU's new Hanseatic League picks its next battle". *Financial Times*, 11 October 2018. https://www.ft.com/content/ca9dc2dc-c52a-11e8-bc21-54264d1c4647.

Khanna, P. "Beyond city limits". *Foreign Policy*, Sep/Oct 2010; https://foreignpolicy.com/2010/08/06/beyond-city-limits/.

Khanna, P. *How to Run the World Charting a Course to the Next Renaissance*. New York: Random House, 2011.

Kickert, W. "Distinctiveness in the study of public management in Europe: a historical institutional analysis of France, Germany and Italy". *Public Management Review* 7:4 (2005): 537–63.

Knaus, G. "Islamic Calvinists". *Prospect Magazine*, 14 January 2007; https://www.prospectmagazine.co.uk/magazine/islamic calvinists.

Koch, H. "Ordet eller Sværdet". *Berlingske Aftenavis*, 12 September 1945; https://danmarkshistorien.dk/leksikon-og-kilder/vis/materiale/hal-koch-ordet-eller-svaerdet-1945/.

Koch, P. & T. Knudsen. *Ansvaret der forsvandt: om magten, ministrene og embedsværket*. Copenhagen: Samfundslitteratur, 2014.

Kopstein, J. "The transatlantic divide over democracy promotion". *Washington Quarterly* 29:2 (2005): 85–98.

Laclau, E. & C. Mouffe. *Hegemony and Socialist Strategy: Towards a Radical Democratic Politics*. London: Verso, 1985.

Lasch, C. *The Culture of Narcissism: American Life in an Age of Diminishing Expectations*. New York: Norton, 1991.

LeGoff, J. *L'Uomo medievale*. Bari: LaTerza, 2006.

Leonard, M. *Why Europe will Run the 21st Century*. London: Fourth Estate, 2005.

Lewis, B. *What Went Wrong? The Clash Between Islam and Modernity in the Middle East*. New York: Harper Perennial, 2012.

Lidegaard B. & F. Tassinari. "The same creed: a conversation about Scandinavian democracy". *OpenDemocracy*, 11 February 2014; https://www.opendemocracy.net/en/can-europe-make-it/same-creed-conversation-about-scandinavian-democr/.

Lindung, Y. "Interview with Michel Foucault". *Bonniers Litteräre Magasin* 37:3 (1968): 203–11.

Linz, J. & A. Stepan. *Problems of Democratic Transition and Consolidation: Southern Europe, South America, and Post-Communist Europe*. Baltimore, MD: Johns Hopkins University Press, 1996.

Local. "'Crawl back under your rock', Swedish foreign minister tells Canadian professor Jordan B Peterson". *The Local*, 11 August 2018; https://www.thelocal.se/20181108/crawl-back-under-your-rock-swedish-foreign-minister-tells-canadian-professor-jordan-peterson/.

Madison, A. *The World Economy: A Millennial Perspective*. Paris: OECD, 2001. http://www.theworldeconomy.org.

Madsen, P. "The Danish model of 'flexicurity': experiences and lessons". *European Review of Labor and Research* 10:2 (2004): 187–207.

Marklund, C. "Hot love and cold people: sexual liberalism as political escapism in radical Sweden". *NORDEUROPAforum* 19:1 (2009): 83–101.

Markowitz, D. *The Meritocracy Trap: How America's Foundational Myth Feeds Inequality, Dismantles the Middle Class, and Devours the Elite.* New York: Penguin, 2019.

Martela, F. *et al.* "The Nordic exceptionalism: what explains why the Nordic countries are constantly among the happiest in the world". World Happiness Report, 20 March 2020; https://worldhappiness.report/ed/2020/the-nordic-exceptionalism-what-explains-why-the-nordic-countries-are-constantly-among-the-happiest-in-the-world/.

Maselli, I. "Flexicurity in Italy – how Far is Rome from Copenhagen?" DIIS Policy Brief, September 2012; http://subweb.diis.dk/graphics/Publications/Policybriefs2012/Flexicurity%20Italy_DIIS%20policy%20brief.screen.pdf.

Matthijs, M. "Mediterranean blues: the crisis in Southern Europe". *Journal of Democracy* 25:1 (2014): 101–15.

Miklian, J. "Rough cut". *Foreign Policy*, 2 January 2013; https://foreignpolicy.com/2013/01/02/rough-cut/.

Milne, R. "Global threat fails to break spirit of Sweden's labour model". *Financial Times*, 6 January 2014; https://www.ft.com/content/4c887088-683f-11e3-8ada-00144feabdc0.

Milne, R. "Architect of Sweden's no-lockdown strategy insists it will pay off". *Financial Times*, 8 May 2020; https://www.ft.com/content/a2b4c18c-a5e8-4edc-8047-ade4a82a548d.

Mokyr, J. "The enduring riddle of the European miracle: the Enlightenment and the Industrial Revolution". Departments of Economics and History, Northwestern University, 2002; http://citeseerx.ist.psu.edu/viewdoc/download?doi=10.1.1.477.6576&rep=rep1&type=pdf.

Monti, M. "Europe's leaders need to back shift on rules on public investment". *Financial Times*, 8 October 2014; https://www.ft.com/content/ba9cd208-4d5e-11e4-bf60-00144feab7de.

Moravcsik, A. "In defense of the 'democratic deficit': reassessing legitimacy in the European Union". Center for European Studies Working Paper No. 92 (1992).

Moravcsik, A. "Europe after the crisis: how to sustain a common currency". *Foreign Affairs* 91:3 (2012): 54–68.

Murray, P. "French notaries and the American mortgage crisis". In M. Rogoff, M. Dixon & E. Bither (eds), *The Financial Crisis of 2008: French and American Responses*. Proceedings of the 2010 Franco-American Legal Seminar, 2011.

Naim, M. "Minilateralism: the magic number to get real international action". *Foreign Policy*, July/Aug 2009; https://foreignpolicy.com/2009/06/21/minilateralism/.

National Intelligence Counci. *Global Governance 2025: At a Critical Juncture*. September 2010.

Neher, C. "Asian style democracy". *Asian Survey* 34:11 (1994): 949–61.

Neumann, I. "Regions in international relations theory: the case for a region-building approach". Oslo: Norwegian Institute of International Affairs, 1992.

Nikel, D. "Why Sweden's coronavirus approach is so different from others". *Forbes*, 30 March 2020; https://www.forbes.com/sites/davidnikel/2020/03/30/why-swedens-coronavirus-approach-is-so-different-from-others/.

Obama, B. President Obama endorses Joe Biden for President. 14 April 2020; https://youtu.be/5-s3ANu4eMs.

OECD. *Society at a Glance 2019: OECD Social Indicators*. Paris: OECD, 2019; https://www.oecd-ilibrary.org/social-issues-migration-health/society-at-a-glance-2019_f0af5150-en.

OECD. "Income inequality". Paris: OECD, 2020.

Ohlsson, P. "Close friends and distant: relations between the United States and Sweden over 200 years". Columbia University, New York, 23 September 2003.

Ohlsson, P. "Sweden: still the middle way?". Columbia University, New York, 28 September 2006.

Olson, M. *How Bright are the Northern Lights? Some Questions about Sweden*. Institute of Economic Research, Lund University, 1990.

Østergaard, U. "Lutheranism, nationalism and the universal welfare state: national churches and national identity after the

Reformation and the development of the welfare state in the Nordic national states". In K. Kunter & J. Holger Schjørring (eds), *Europäisches und globales Christentum: Herausforderungen und Transformationen im 20. Jahrhundert*. Gottingen: Vandenhoeck & Ruprecht, 2011.

Packer, G. "The broken contract". *Foreign Affairs*, Nov/Dec 2011; https://www.foreignaffairs.com/articles/united-states/2011-10-11/broken-contract.

Paterlini, M. "'Closing borders is ridiculous': the epidemiologist behind Sweden's controversial coronavirus strategy". *Nature*, 21 April 2020; https://www.nature.com/articles/d41586-020-01098-x.

Pellegrino, B. & L. Zingales. "Diagnosing the Italian disease". Research paper, Chicago Booth Business School, University of Chicago, 2017; http://faculty.chicagobooth.edu/luigi.zingales/papers/research/Diagnosing.pdf.

Pettersson, V. 1948. "Ancient and modern Swedish land tenure policy". *Journal of Farm Economics* 30:2 (1948): 322–31.

Ponte, S. & L.-A. Richey. *Brand Aid: Shopping Well to Save the World*. Minneapolis, MN: University of Minnesota Press, 2011.

Pope Pious XI. *Encyclical Quadrigesimo Anno*. Vatican City, 1931.

Pritchett, L. & M. Woolcock. "Solutions when the solution is the problem: arraying the disarray in development". *World Development* 32:2 (2004): 191–212.

Przeworski, A. & F. Limongi. "Modernization: theories and facts". *World Politics* 49:2 (1997): 155–83.

Putnam, R. *et al. Making Democracy Work: Civic Traditions in Modern Italy*. Princeton, NJ: Princeton University Press, 1993.

Queen Margaret II. "H.M. Dronning Margrethe II's nytårstale". https://dansketaler.dk/tale/dronningens-nytaarstale-2003/.

Rachman, G. "Indian democracy has an ugly side". *Financial Times*, 18 May 2009.

Rachman, G. *Zero-Sum World: Politics, Power and Prosperity After the Crash*. London: Atlantic, 2010.

Radjou, N. "India: the emerging innovation giant". Council on Foreign Relations, 14 October 2008.

Ramo, J. "The Beijing consensus". London, Foreign Policy Centre, May 2004; https://fpc.org.uk/wp-content/uploads/2006/09/244.pdf/.

Ramo, J. *The Age of the Unthinkable: Why the New World Disorder Constantly Surprises Us And What We Can Do About It.* New York: Little Brown, 2009.

Rasmussen, M. *A Time for Peace: The West, Civil Society and the Construction of Peace Following the First World War, the Second World War and the Cold War.* Copenhagen: Political Studies Press, 2001.

Rifkin, J. *The European Dream: How Europe's Vision of the Future is Quietly Eclipsing the American Dream.* Cambridge: Polity, 2004.

Rizzo, S. & G. Stella. *La casta. Perché i politici italiani continuano a essere intoccabili.* Milan: Rizzoli, 2007.

Rothstein, B. *Social Traps and the Problem of Trust.* Cambridge: Cambridge University Press, 2005.

Said, E. *Orientalism.* New York: Doubleday, 1978.

Samans, R., K. Schwab & M. Malloch-Brown. "Running the world, after the crash". *Foreign Policy,* Jan/Feb 2011; https://foreignpolicy.com/2011/01/03/running-the-world-after-the-crash/.

Schultheis, E. "What right-wing populists look like in Norway can they avoid the nativism of their European peers?" *The Atlantic,* September 2017; https://www.theatlantic.com/international/archive/2017/09/norway-progress-party-populism-immigration/539535/.

Simovska, V. & P. McNamara (eds). *Schools for Health and Sustainability: Theory, Research and Practice.* Berlin: Springer, 2015.

Skinner, Q. "Ambrogio Lorenzetti: the artist as political philosopher". Raleigh Lecture on History. London: British Academy, 1986.

Smith, P. *Just Kids.* London: Bloomsbury, 2010.

Sontag, S. "A letter from Sweden". *Ramparts Magazine,* July 1969: 23–38.

Stavinoha, L. & A. Fotiadis. "Asylum outsourced: McKinsey's secret role in Europe's refugee crisis". *Balkan Insight,* 22 June 2020;

https://balkaninsight.com/2020/06/22/asylum-outsourced-mckinseys-secret-role-in-europes-refugee-crisis/.

Stephen, C. "Comment: Milosevic and the Al Capone dimension". Institute for War & Peace Reporting, 22 February 2005; https://iwpr.net/global-voices/comment-milosevic-and-al-capone-dimension.

Svanborg Sjövall, K. "Privatising the Swedish welfare state". *Economic Affairs* 34:2 (2014): 181–92.

Taleb, N. *The Black Swan: The Impact of the Highly Improbable.* London: Allen Lane, 2007.

Tassinari, F. "Mario Monti's Nordic dream". *Project Syndicate*, May 2012; https://www.project-syndicate.org/commentary/mario-monti-s-nordic-dream?barrier=accesspaylog.

Tassinari, F. & S. Miller. "Nordic cuddly capitalism: cover story". *Christian Science Monitor*, 11 May 2014.

Tassinari, F. & L. Vissing. "Living in denial: the cultural factor in European policies and politics". DIIS Working Papers, 2017: 3; https://www.jstor.org/stable/resrep13402?seq=1#metadata_info_tab_contents.

Telegraph. "Chinese Premier Wen Jiabao: democracy in China is 'inevitable'". *The Telegraph*, 14 March 2012.

Toschi, P. "Italy's Jobs Act passes the first hurdle". *JP Morgan Commentary and Analysis*, 9 October 2014; http://insights.jpmorgan.co.uk/assetmanager/commentary-and-analysis/italys-jobs-act-passes-the-first-hurdle/.

Totaro, L. "Italy's Renzi wins vote on controversial labor law change". Bloomberg News, 8 October 2014; https://www.bloomberg.com/news/articles/2014-10-08/italy-s-renzi-wins-vote-on-controversial-labor-law-change.

Tracy, B. "High stakes for Calif. Prop 30 Election Day decision". CBS News, 6 November 2012; https://www.cbsnews.com/news/high-stakes-for-calif-prop-30-election-day-decision/.

REFERENCES

Transparency International. Corruption Perception Index 2019. https://www.transparency.org/files/content/pages/2019_CPI_Report_EN.pdf.

Truman, E. *Sovereign Wealth Funds: Threat or Salvation?* Washington, DC: Peterson Institute for International Economics, 2009.

Tynell, J. *Mørkelygten.* Copenhagen: SamfundsLitteratur, 2016.

University of Gothenburg. Quality of Government Index 2012; https://www.gu.se/en/quality-government/qog-data/data-downloads/european-quality-of-government-index.

Valery, P. "Disillusionment" (1919). http://www.historymuse.net/readings/ValeryDISILLUSIONMENT.htm.

Vidal, J. & S. Goldenberger. "Snowden revelations of NSA spying on Copenhagen climate talks spark anger". *The Guardian,* 31 January 2014; http://www.theguardian.com/environment/2014/jan/30/snowden-nsa-spying-copenhagen-climate-talks

Vogel, E. *Deng Xiaoping and the Transformation of China.* Cambridge, MA: Harvard University Press, 2013.

Waever, O. "European security identities". *Journal of Common Market Studies* 34:1 (1996): 103–32.

Waever, O. "Security, the speech act: analysing the politics of a word". Center for Peace and Conflict Research Working Paper no. 2, 1989.

Walt, S. "International relations: one world many theories". *Foreign Policy* 110 (1998): 29–32, 34–46.

Walt, V. "Diamonds aren't forever". *Fortune,* 7 December 2006; https://money.cnn.com/magazines/fortune/fortune_archive/2006/12/11/8395442/index.htm.

Watson, A. *The Evolution of International Society: A Comparative Historical Analysis.* London: Routledge, 1992.

Weber, M. *Economy and Society: An Outline of Interpretive Sociology* [1922]. Los Angeles, CA: University of California Press, 1978.

Wendt, A. "Anarchy is what states make of it: the social construction of power politics". *International Organization* 46:2 (1992): 391–425.

Westerwinter, O. The Politics of Transnational Institutions: Power, Bargaining and Institutional Choice. PhD dissertation, European University Institute, Florence, 2014.

Williams, M. & R. Abrahamsen. *Security Beyond the State: Private Security in International Politics*. Cambridge: Cambridge University Press, 2011.

Wilson, A. *Virtual Politics: Faking Democracy in the Post-Soviet World.* New Haven, CT: Yale University Press, 2005.

Wolf, M. "Lunch with the FT: Francis Fukuyama". *Financial Times*, 27 May 2011.

Woodward, V. *The Comparative Approach to American History*. Oxford: Oxford University Press, 1997.

World Bank. *Worldwide Governance Indicators*. Washington, DC: World Bank, 2012.

World Economic Forum. "Rebuilding Europe's competitiveness". Geneva, 2013.

World Economic Forum. "Which countries tax their citizens the most?" Geneva, 2019.

World Economic Forum. *The Global Competitiveness Report*. Geneva, 2019. http://www3.weforum.org/docs/WEF_TheGlobal CompetitivenessReport2019.pdf.

Wright, C. "Tackling conflict diamonds: the Kimberley Process certification scheme". *International Peacekeeping* 11:4 (2004): 697–708.

Yin, R. *Case Study Research: Design and Methods*. London: Sage, 1989.

Zakaria, F. "Culture is destiny: a conversation with Lee Kwan Yew". *Foreign Affairs* 73:2 (1994): 109–26.

Zakaria, F. "The rise of illiberal democracy". *Foreign Affairs* 76:6 (1997): 22–43.

Zakaria, F. *The Future of Freedom: Illiberal Democracy at Home and Abroad.* New York: Norton, 2003.

Zakaria, F. *The Post-American World.* New York: Norton, 2008.

Index